Romancing the *Stove*

Romancing *the* Stove

Celebrated Recipes and Delicious Fun for Every Kitchen Goddess

Margie Lapanja

Foreword by Andrew F. Smith

Conari Press

ISBN: 1-57324-858-4

Cover Design: Maxine Ressler
Cover Photography: © C Squared Studios/PictureQuest,
                    © Renzo Mancini/Getty Images

This has been previously cataloged by the Library of Congress under this title
Lapanja, Margaret Beiser,
     Goddess in the kitchen: 201 heavenly recipes, spirited stories &
saucy secrets / by Margie Lapanja.
          p.   cm.
     Includes index.
     ISBN 1-57324-115-6
     1. Cookery.   I. Title.
TX714.L345   1998
641.5—dc21   98-4612

Printed in Canada on recycled paper.

02 03 04 05 TC 10 9 8 7 6 5 4 3 2 1

To
Dorismarie Welcher
"Queen of the Hudson"

Colorful goddess, zesty mentor, and
quintessential friend, who taught me this:

believe and receive;

doubt and lose out.

Life is a glorious banquet,
a limitless and delicious buffet.

MAYA ANGELOU

Contents

Foreword

When is the last time you picked up a cookbook and actually read it from cover to cover? I don't mean skimmed some recipes, I mean really read a cookbook? For me, it had been a long while until I encountered Margie Lapanja's *Romancing the Stove*. It is one of the few modern cookery books that I actually read—and relished—from beginning to end. In fact, I read it twice. My initial reason for reading the entire book was to immerse myself in the stories, commentary and pithy quotes. As a culinary historian, I must admit that I was looking for historical fallacies and errors. Foiled in this initial quest, I found that I enjoyed her chatty, informal, conversational style. Her playful, sensual, lightly-historical approach is a delight. This cookbook is filled with enchanting commentary and wonderful stories, along with recipes that would please the goddesses (and gods).

Margie Lapanja's selection of pithy quotes is gleaned from a wide variety of sources—the Bible, Chinese, Irish and Italian proverbs to Shakespeare and Moliere, and from Goethe, Blake, Twain and Emerson to Michael Jordan and Toni Morrison. (If you don't recognize all the people she quotes—don't worry, neither did I.) Sage snippets of wisdom are laced with witty interludes of that old-time, down-to-earth Midwestern good sense and sensibility. At the other end of the intellectual spectrum is the practical culinary advice that I will surely use when the need arises. All in all, this is a fun-filled book packed with unexpected gastronomical pleasures.

While *Romancing the Stove's* approach to modern cookbook writing may appear a bit unusual, it falls well within the traditions of the art form. Since the first cookbook,

Platina's *De honesta voluptate* (in case your Latin is rusty, this is translated "Concerning Honest Pleasure"), was published in Venice in 1475 cookbooks have been closely associated with sensual pleasures, ancient Greek and Roman gods and goddesses, as well as culinary delights and good recipes. All pleasures were connected, and gastronomical pleasures were no exceptions. Of course, during the Renaissance few cooks could read, and so the culinary works were really aimed at the literate, upperclass elite.

During the centuries that followed, the cookbook field went in three directions. One direction was geared toward the professionalization of cookery. These cookbooks were written by the professional chef for professional chefs. Mainly written by French and Italian masters, such as Bartolomeo Scappi's and Pierre François de la Varenne's works, these cookbooks stand today as exemplars of culinary masterpieces much as do the works art of Michelangelo or Leonardo da Vinci. Alas, this golden age of literary cookbooks was not to last.

The second direction was exemplified by cookbooks written by men telling women what to do in the kitchen. Their comments about women and women's roles in life were highly influenced by Puritanical values which today can be relegated to the historical dustbin. Their recipes are most interesting as little evidence suggests that few of these authors ever made it into the kitchen themselves to test out their proposed instructions.

The third direction was toward the practical guidance based on rich experience gained in the kitchen. Not surprisingly, these were written mainly by women. Some of the best cookbooks ever written fall into this category, such as Hannah Glasse's *The Art of Cookery* (London, 1747) and Mary Randolph's *The Virginia Housewife* (Washington, 1824).

Somewhere in the late nineteenth century, the art of cookery turned into a pseudo-science, consisting of a compilation of chemistry-like formulae filled with ingredients, weights, measures, temperatures, vitamins, proteins, carbohydrates and durations. Cookbooks also tended to become much simpler, because the authors themselves were not cooks. The writers, best exemplified by Fannie Farmer's *Boston Cooking-School Cook Book* (Boston, 1896), assumed that their target reader did not know how to cook, but could follow simple laboratory-like directions.

With the scientific and simplistic approaches ensconced in the kitchen, all other distractions disappeared from cookbooks. Literary references were removed; comments about life excluded; and the sensual connections were banned. Sadly, one of the distractions was the fun of cookery and of cookbook writing.

Margie Lapanja's *Romancing the Stove* successfully combines a variety of elements of cookbooks of the past. She demonstrates the qualities of the professional chef and offers excellent cooking tips. She reintroduces the ancient philosophical wisdom and modern culinary insight. Unlike the earlier cookbook authors who were completely serious about their references to the geniuses of the past, Margie Lapanja weaves them into the text with joy and lightheartedness. This contrasts with many of our predispositions, in the face of harried modern life, that cookery is a boring drudgery and a necessary evil. Putting the playfulness back into cooking is one of the book's most charming messages.

It was only after I read the book the first time that I went back to peruse the recipes carefully. These heavenly creations appeared to merit attention in their own right. But titillating titles and incredible ingredients do not necessarily a good recipe make. Now, let me be honest: in the kitchen, no goddess am I. Although I have been known to dabble a bit in the kitchen, by no stretch of the imagination am I a great cook. However, spirited with Margie Lapanja's recipes, I imagined myself in the kitchen with the goddesses Demeter, Artemis and Aphrodite and explored several of the dishes. Of course, as a true tomato lover, I had to try "Love Apple Linguini," which was as good as

I anticipated. I noshed on "Norwegian Oatmeal Waffles," munched "Mandarin Spinach Salad," chomped on "Curry Sweet Potatoes with Chicken Apple Sausage," and nibbled on "Magic Double Fudge Brownies." (As a brownie afficionado I rate this last recipe as one of the finer examples of the art.) I'm looking forward to exploring them all.

While Margie Lapanja's *Romancing the Stove* rests on the solid foundation of the past, I suspect that this cookbook will be in use and in print for a long time to come.

—Andrew F. Smith, culinary historian, editor-in-chief of *Oxford University Press Encyclopedia of American Food and Drink*, and author of *The Tomato in America*, *Pure Ketchup*, *Popped Culture*, and *Peanuts: The Illustrious History of the Goober Pea*

CHAPTER 1

Good Goddess, Let's Eat!

THE KITCHEN GODDESS MANIFESTO

Kitchen Goddess:

a luminary;

a person who enlightens others through her grace and craft;

a woman whose charm and cooking arouse adoration.

Her motto:

Eat dessert first!

*O*nce upon a time, when I was a child playing make-believe with my Susie Homemaker light bulb-powered oven, I daydreamed I was a spell-mixing sibyl who could concoct magic love potions. The Fates seemed to seal this childhood fantasy when, some twenty-odd years later, I found myself the proprietor of a popular bakery in California.

During my many years as a professional baker, I observed the seductive effects of food on the human psyche and soul. Hearts and palates beamed when offered birthday cakes, wedding cakes, hot, heart-warming strudels, homemade applesauce, and of course, the ultimate love potion—cookies. Over and over, certain foods seemed to cohere relationships, mend broken hearts, and energize athletes to the point of victory. Clearly some foods possess magical qualities—and I wanted to capture that magnetism.

As time went on and I saw the magic happen over and over, I asked people to tell me about their most favorite food and explain why it was sacred to them. As I collected, tested, revised, and retested these favorite recipes, I took care to prepare each in the same spirit of its owner's spicy love or grounding tradition. In 1991, I sold my cookie business and packed my recipes in a suitcase until I had time to write a cookbook.

But the spell-binding aspect of food continued to captivate me. When everyone else jumped on the Martha Stewart bandwagon, raising spotless, cut-glass, antique crystal goblets in a toast to perfection, I remained loyal to my favorite kitchen courtesan of all time—Samantha Stevens, the blithe, blond enchantress of the television classic, *Bewitched*. With a quick twitch of the nose, she could certainly stir it up! With this in mind, I raised my measuring cup to her and learned to "wiggle my nose." Having a grand time in the kitchen whipping up "spells" was certainly fun! When people began telling me my cookies tasted better than Mrs. Fields', I began to playfully fancy myself a "Grace Kelly of the kitchen" and laced my cooking with a good measure of class and charisma—

I was never destined to be an average, mortal, commoner cook . . . Then it hit me—
I was a kitchen goddess!

A kitchen goddess is a food sensualist who honors every aspect of creating a meal, from choosing the raw ingredients to artfully blending them and serving them with unique panache—be it *coq au vin* that took three hours to prepare or a two-minute peanut butter and jelly sandwich. A kitchen goddess moves through life with a buoyant and reassured attitude and *knows* it is her culinary responsibility to play and have fun. In particular, she's not afraid of food: Rather than anxiously counting calories and fat grams, she basks in the beauty of a fresh lime, the succulence of a ripe pear, the crispness of a chocolate chip cookie. She embraces any challenge with a *sans souci* spirit that is cradled deeply within an open-hearted, secure love for herself, her friends, and her family. She makes mealtimes a sacred connecting experience for those around her, and her food offerings flow from a sense of generosity, not obligation. She blesses the moment with her presence.

For too long, women have been burdened with the three-meal-a-day obligation, losing their sense of the joy of cooking under the endless expectations of hungry families. For many, cooking has come to be seen as drudgery at best, an anxiety-provoking experience at worst. And with performance pressure whispering "perfection" at every turn, an unsettling feeling of domestic deficiency has crept into many a kitchen.

We now know it doesn't have to be that way—we can reclaim our connection to the divine feminine and to the playful, sensuous experience that cooking can be. Cooking doesn't have to be a chore or a social-status do-it-perfectly experience; the time has come to *energize* and *personalize* cooking and *relax* while mixing up marvelous concoctions. Becoming a kitchen goddess is easy. All it takes is a certain attitude, a pinch of love, and a few great recipes. Believe this: A special, desired dish, prepared and served with love and your best intentions, possesses the power to brighten the world.

Goddesses of Yore

*I*n mythology, the goddess was a woman of intuitive knowledge, numinous power, and abiding wisdom. Revered, honored, held in awe, sometimes feared, she was the divine feminine personified in her many forms: Aphrodite, the alchemical goddess of creativity, passion, and love; Demeter, the Earth-Mother goddess of grains and the nourishment of the soul; Artemis, the wild woman-sister goddess of the forest, the moon, and the hunt; Vesta, the maiden wise woman and goddess of the hearth and home; Hera, the queen of contracts, marriage, and order; Persephone, the vulnerable goddess of the night; and Athena, daddy's girl and the goddess of wisdom, victory in conflict, and worldly knowledge.

But my question is, could they cook?

And if so, what would be their legacies in the kitchen?

Aphrodite would certainly stir up some tried-and-true love potions, such as aromatic apple pies; Hera would leap into the role of the culinary bellwether Martha Stewart; and Artemis would probably give ferociously festive and untamed dinner parties for her women friends—and a few brave, well-behaved men. Persephone might graciously and demurely pass on cooking altogether, preferring to eat pomegranates and take-out by the light of the half-moon; Vesta and her Greek doppelgänger, Hestia, would stay home alone and indulge in secret, satisfying pleasures; Demeter, Ceres to the Romans, would feed the kids, bake some bread, and keep great reserves of her beloved signature dish—cereal—on hand in the cupboard; Athena would hire a caterer.

It is in the spirit of these gallivanting gourmets that I invite you to explore your own *thealogy* of the goddess in the kitchen, and encourage you to infuse your knowledge of the culinary crafts with your own inspired brand of humor and genius. You might lean toward the style of earth-mother Demeter and make huge meals for loved ones. Or you might be more of an Aphrodite, saving cooking for special romantic occasions. Or perhaps, day by day, your affinities change. Whatever your tendency, I urge you to embrace it fully, to explore its myriad possibilities in the kitchen.

In this light, I have cooked up *Romancing the Stove*. This zesty collection of feel-good favorites and free-flying fun is dedicated to every one of you, kitchen goddesses and demigods, who are ready to roll up your sleeves, "face the stove," and start waving your mixing-spoon scepters.

To begin, post the following on your refrigerator—*If you ever wish to add to the happiness of another individual, simply ask, "What is your favorite food, drink, or dessert?"—then serve it forth.*

Preparing food and cooking it with the flair of a kitchen goddess can be a grounding, spiritual, art form, especially when you have recipes that are:

* *legendary in effect*
* *pleasurable to make*
* *not too much work*
* *expressive and creative*
* *what people love to eat*

When consumed, these foods will never make you or anyone else fat, will always taste good, and will bring about smiles; even the preparation will add delicious fun and a *joie de vivre* to an otherwise mundane kitchen. And, best of all, you'll forever stop comparing your talents with those of Martha or your husband's mother.

In order to really be a goddess in the kitchen, it's essential to embrace a few basic attitudes and behaviors. They will all make cooking and eating more fun, but the first rule is essential.

The Kitchen Goddess Manifesto

1. Do not cook if you are in a bad mood, lack the desire, or feel pressure from nagging obligation to another. Wise woman Brenda Ueland once said, "Do not do anything you don't want to do." Frame this mantra and hang it where you'll read it every day. And remember—you can always go out, order take-out, or entice someone else to host a cook out.

2. Keep your life full of the freshest ingredients. At least once a week explore something completely new: A new recipe . . . a new book . . . an unfamiliar song. Try new things: Make a new friend . . . dance outdoors . . . take a walk somewhere you have never been before . . . kiss a baby . . . write to someone you admire and include a favorite recipe . . . *talk* to someone who doesn't speak your language . . .

3. *Delighten* up and play with your cooking! Read the recipe, then have fun! The more you play, the more you do what you love to do, the more you reconnect with your talents and power.

4. *Always* sit down when you eat; share most of your meals if you can.

5. Customize your creations and spice them with your own unique delicious hallmarks. As the saying goes, "Don't be the best at what you do; be the only one who does what you do."

6. Take a deep breath and bless your kitchen before you cook; clean up all rampant clutter, light a candle, open a window, turn on music. When in the mood,

pour your favorite drink, be it wine, water, whiskey, or an ice-cold root beer in a frosted mug.

7. When recipes are given to you, save the original in the handwriting of the person who shared the recipe; he or she will be honored this way. Create a beautiful binder of recipes in sheet protectors for your collection. If you want to frolic and improvise, rewrite your new recipe on a page next to the original.

8. Never, *ever* think that food will make you fat! Delete the words "fat-free" and "sugar-free" from your culinary vocabulary and replace them with "fear-free," "guilt-free," and *"feel free!"*

9. Whenever you taste something that sparks your spirit and your taste buds, ask for the recipe. Trade, beg, or borrow—but get it.

10. Trust yourself, and have fun.

I don't like to say that my kitchen is a religious place,
but I would say that if I were a voodoo princess,
I would conduct my rituals there.

—Pearl Bailey

Serve It Forth

*A*rmed with the Kitchen Goddess Manifesto, let your kitchen be a *play-ground* where culinary magic is shared and enjoyed, evolving with time and tastes. A goddess in the kitchen feels free to alter and enhance recipes and simply *frolic* while cooking; she knows that it is often the serendipitous approach that creates a masterpiece.

Now step into your kitchen and cook with a confident, inspired *élan vital*. If you sprinkle illuminated thoughts, wishes, and desires into your mixing bowl, you'll provide fertile nutrition for the spirit and mind as well as for the body and taste buds. As you begin to radiate a refreshing presence of enthusiasm, energy, and joy between the counter and the stove, the light will pour out into the world around you. Kids, friends, and mates will all want to join you in your domain.

Don't be afraid to create your own traditions—through the power of suggestion, your specialties will become legendary. You'll smile knowingly when you hear that people are *still* talking about that Garden of Eden Apple Pie or Casablanca Cheesecake you brought to the party!

Kitchen play can serve as a lively springboard for exploring a multitude of talents and other goddess-given gifts. With this treasure trove of rollicking recipes, spicy advice, and entertaining insights, I invite you all to do a front-flip dive into the spirited, sensuous art of cooking, loving, and living. Just as Aphrodite stirred up history with her legacy of unabashed passion and love, you have the opportunity to stir up your own brand of culinary magic.

The goddess is in every kitchen. Join me now as we heat up a caldron of delicious fun and serve ourselves some passion-provoking "food of the goddess."

A Goddess in Any Other Kitchen

Basque ... *jainkosa*

Danish ... *gudinde*

Dutch ... *godin*

Finnish ... *jumalatar*

French ... *déesse*

Gaelic ... *ban-dia*

German ... *Göttin*

Hawaiian ... *akua wahine*

Serbo-Croatian ... *božica*

Spanish ... *diosa*

Swedish ... *gudinna*

Tagalog (Philipino) ... *diwata*

Thai ... *tep-ti-da*

Turkish ... *tanriça*

Latin ... *dea*

Lithuanian ... *deivě*

Malay ... *dewi*

Norwegian ... *gudinne*

Polish ... *bogini*

Portuguese ... *deusa*

Romanian ... *zeiţă*

Slovene ... *boginja*

Irish ... *bandia*

Indonesian ... *dewi*

Italian ... *dea*

Japanese ... *me ga mi*

Korean ... *yŏ-sin*

Vietnamese ... *nū-thần*

CHAPTER 2

Demeter's Delights

HEARTWARMING
TREASURES
FOR THE KID
IN ALL OF US

*D*emeter, the great goddess of grain, was the kind of doting mother who would have indulged us with the magic that comes with hot, homemade cookies, a big glass of milk, and long, loving hugs. She would see to it that our lives and plates were chock-full of all the sustaining staples that keep kids feeling safe. We would learn from her that it really is never too late to have a happy childhood, that chicken soup really does make you feel better, and that the sun always rises, bringing into each new day a fresh measure of enchantment and accomplishment.

As legend has it, Demeter was distraught and heartbroken over losing her daughter Persephone, who was abducted by Hades and made queen-consort of the Underworld. In her sadness, Demeter donned an emotional version of a full-length apron to disguise her radiant beauty and wandered in desperation, refusing to cook or brush her hair, searching for her abducted daughter. Amber waves of grain were scorched to the ground and a blight of famine and drought descended upon the earth.

This mighty mama was not to settle for being a victim, however. Upon finding that Zeus, her indiscreet brother and the father of Persephone (oops), had done some dirty dealing with Hades, promising Persephone as the prize, Demeter fumed. As tough mothers can do, she put her divine foot down and forced Zeus into a compromise: When the grain was in the ground, heralding eight months of lush fertility and nourishment, Persephone would be with her beloved mother and the gifts of fruitfulness and abundance would shine over the lands. But for four months of the year when Persephone was with Hades in the shadowed netherworld, Demeter's earth would lie barren, devoid of life.

And so the grain goddess regained her cherished role of mother. To pass the time without her daughter, she was known to lavish other children with her attentions. She tried to immortalize the babe Demophon by feeding and massaging him with ambrosia while holding him close to a fire, warming the mortality right out of him. We can only imagine what she cooked for him.

In the name of the supermom Demeter, and in honor of children of all ages, I offer these time-tested, smile-raising recipes for some of life's sweetest treats, let's-eat-with-our-fingers fun foods, the heart-warming, hug-filled favorites of childhood.

In a true sense, a cookbook is the best source of psychological advice
and the kitchen the first choice of room for a therapy of the world.

—Thomas Moore, *The Re-Enchantment of Everyday Life*

Prescription for a Playful Palate

Next time you are feeling desperately overextended with obligations, deadlines, work, concern, and unfulfilled responsibility, remember that there are such things in life as Cookie Dough Pancakes. These little islets of lumpy, puffy, flapjacks in a sea of grown-up worries have the power to transform muddled tension into childhood bliss. It takes only a few bites. Just allow yourself to imagine the delicious feeling of triumph over those brow-furrowing issues trying to knock you off balance.

To eat a Cookie Dough Pancake you have to glide into a fairly naughty state of conditional anarchy—you are challenging the breakfast establishment when biting into this territory. Raw cookie dough at breakfast? Forbidden! Yet, when enveloped in a hearty, wholesome breakfast pancake, with mom or dad or the little angel sitting on your shoulder flipping it, it transcends all restriction and becomes one of the most-fun-to-eat foods in the universe.

Cookie Dough Pancakes

1 cup buttermilk

1 egg

3 tablespoons butter, melted

½ teaspoon salt

¾ cup unbleached white flour

¾ teaspoon baking soda

½ teaspoon baking powder

Oil for griddle

Powdered sugar, optional

Maple syrup

¾ cup cookie dough, homemade or packaged (I recommend the Royal Oatmeal Raisin Cookie dough on page 50)

In a large bowl, beat the buttermilk and egg together. Add the melted butter and salt and mix well. In a medium bowl, measure out the flour and blend the baking soda and baking powder into it. Add the flour mixture to the buttermilk and mix everything together.

When you are ready to make the pancakes, lightly grease a griddle or pan and heat on medium heat. Without stirring, ladle batter from the bottom of the bowl and pour onto the griddle forming 4-inch pancakes. Drop ½-teaspoon measures of cookie dough onto the pancakes. When the surface of the pancake is covered with bubbles, flip it and cook for another minute.

Dust with powdered sugar or serve with real maple syrup.

Makes a dozen 4-inch pancakes.

A LA GODDESS

* This batter will hold its form if refrigerated for a day or two. However, do not stir it very much before cooking; simply spoon it from the bottom of the bowl. Always add the cookie dough at baking time. If you use homemade dough and are concerned about bacteria in raw eggs, either freeze the dough before you use it or prepare the cookie dough recipe with the proper amount of pasteurized liquid eggs.

* Be creative with this "building batter"—add fruit, berries, or other assorted goodies. I highly recommend lacing it with M&Ms or chocolate chips. Try making "pancake faces" with these or with raisins. Have fun!

A Perfectly Friendly Taste-Tickler

*A*s we know, pumpkin has been canonized in the form of the pumpkin pie. Because this squash matures and is harvested in the coolness of the fall, we have come regard it as autumnal fare, compartmentalizing its use to the time between the fall equinox and New Year's Day. Think about it—do you recall having pumpkin pie in February or May or August? Before the days of Libby's canned pumpkin, obtaining the fruit of fresh equinoctial pumpkin was essential, but now we can conjure the magic of this plump, friendly vegetable any time during the year. And, tell the truth—how many of you use fresh pumpkin for baking, anyway?

The Great Pumpkin Spice Muffins

4 cups unbleached white flour

1¾ cups brown sugar

2 teaspoons baking soda

1½ teaspoons ground cinnamon

1 teaspoon ground nutmeg

1 teaspoon salt

¾ teaspoon ground cloves

4 eggs, beaten

½ cup milk

½ cup yogurt or buttermilk

½ cup water

2 cups cooked pumpkin, fresh or canned

1 ripe banana, mashed

2 tablespoons blackstrap molasses

1 cup raisins

Preheat the oven to 350°F. In a large bowl, blend the flour, sugar, baking soda, cinnamon, nutmeg, salt, and cloves together. In another bowl, whisk together the eggs, milk, yogurt, water, pumpkin, mashed banana, and molasses. Pour the wet ingredients into the dry and stir gently. Fold in the raisins.

Spoon the batter into paper-lined muffin tins. Bake for 20 to 25 minutes or until a wooden toothpick inserted into the center comes out clean. These moist muffins freeze well and reheat beautifully.

Makes 16 standard or 12 monster muffins.

A la Goddess

* Instead of raisins, feel free to add 1 cup fresh or frozen fruit, such as blueberries or sweet cherries. You may also substitute 1½ cups honey (mixing it with the wet ingredients in the process) for the brown sugar. I usually adorn the top of the muffins with brown or raw sugar and/or chopped nuts for a more decorative effect.

I was thinking about the origin of the word pumpkin.
It's such a cute word. Kind of plump and friendly—
and sexy in a farmer's daughter sort of way.

—Tom Robbins, *Still Life with Woodpecker*

*It was her completely loving creative being that was
the complete source of all living.*

—Gertrude Stein

Lila's "Weejan" Waffles

Officially renamed by my daughter when she was a bubbly, bilingual two-year-old (she speaks her mind in Slovene, too!), these maple syrup-drenched wonders are the simplest and most desired breakfast concoctions in our world. Satisfying, superhealthy, and delicious, they make a favorite breakfast-in-hand for an on-the-go, exuberant toddler or an appealing breakfast in bed for a luxuriating adult. You can freeze them and toast them, and, refrigerated, the batter lasts for days (just add a bit of milk if it gets too thick). I always mix them up the night before and grill them in an iron that turns out heart-shaped waffles. These are Demeter's darlings when it comes to generating a smiling stomach, heart, and spirit.

Norwegian Oatmeal Waffles

2 cups milk

2 cups oats (old-fashioned or quick)

2 eggs, separated

2 tablespoons honey or brown sugar

2 tablespoons applesauce

2 tablespoons canola oil or soft butter

½ cup whole wheat flour

½ cup unbleached white flour

1 tablespoon baking powder

½ teaspoon salt

Grease and preheat a waffle iron. Either scald milk in medium saucepan over low heat and pour in oats, or mix milk and oats together in a large bowl and microwave at HIGH for 3 to 4 minutes. Whisk in egg yolks, honey or brown sugar, applesauce, and oil or butter.

In a medium bowl, blend the salt and baking powder into flour. Gently mix the dry and wet ingredients together. Beat the egg whites until they form peaks, and gently fold them into the batter.

Ladle batter into the waffle iron and bake until the indicator light tells you the waffles are done. Serve with all the adornments—sweet butter, maple syrup, and/ or fresh berries—or however you desire.

Makes 8 medium waffles.

A la Goddess

* I always prepare the batter the night before and leave it covered at room temperature. If you do this, you have two options for the eggs:

    Do not separate the eggs—just mix them in all at once, *or*

    Refrigerate the egg whites; whisk and add them right before you cook the waffles.

* Fold your favorite cut-up fresh fruit, such as papaya, blueberries, or peaches, into the batter before you cook the waffles.

The Right Tool for the Right Job

Need I say more? When creating fabulous food, there is a factor equally as important as having skill and a good recipe for guidance: the right tool. When assembling your arsenal of cooking utensils, go first class. You can find quality and value in cookware at commercial or wholesale equipment outlets or by ordering through a wholesale distributor (make friends with someone who owns a restaurant; often they won't mind tossing in an extra order for you in exchange for a huge batch of Cowboy Cookies). I absolutely could not be without these cherished items:

* Commercial-quality baking parchment. To obtain it, I usually go to the bakery department of my local supermarket, and short of pleading, ask the baker to share twenty or thirty sheets with me. It costs them nothing (less than one-fourth cent a piece), but I usually offer to pay, say five cents a sheet. You can also purchase it in rolls. One cannot bake cookies and breads properly without it.

* A commercial quality one- to two-ounce ice cream scoop for scooping cookies and muffins. These can be found at a baker's supply store, but my favorite scoops are Syscoware stainless steel scoops sold through Sysco Food Suppliers (you'll have to purchase this item through a food establishment that contracts with these suppliers—use your charm and imagination). I have had the same scoop for almost twenty years.

* Commercial-quality baking and sauté pans. Heart-shaped baking pans are among my favorite kitchen-goddess aids. I also am a purist when it comes to waffle irons. A good waffle iron is as important as the batter; I own several. A top-shelf

Belgian iron (also called a "new Belgian waffler") and a five-heart classic that has heavy plates and heats evenly are treasures, and can usually be found at or ordered through specialty gourmet cooking stores, such as Williams-Sonoma (800-541-2233).

* A thirteen-quart stainless steel mixing bowl. Bowls of this capacity can hold most recipes with ease. Add a nice, sturdy, long-handled mixing spoon (French-made are the best), and you'll be ready to stir it up!

It seems to me that our three basic needs—for food and
security and love—are so mixed and mingled and entwined
that we cannot straightly think of one without the other.

—M. F. K. Fisher

Energy is delight.

—Blake

Stirring Up a Wish Come True

The word *wish* is derived from the Indo-European base word *wen*, meaning to strive for or desire, and is akin to the word *win*, which, according to my dictionary, somehow vibrates to the Latin *venus*, love. The meaning is universal: to have a deep longing for; want; desire; crave. Add to this a teaspoon of hope, a tablespoon of good fortune, and a pinch of faith. Stir it all together, simmer with focused attention, unfaltering intention, and voilà! Wishing Soup.

Special foods often act as a symbolic manifestation of an internal desire or belief system. Cookies, cakes, and soups top the list of these divine potions for the soul and imagination. Consider the *Chicken Soup for the Soul* series of books; the name alone gives us the warm fuzzies that we so crave, that all-encompassing Demeter/mother-love that a big, steaming bowl of soup represents to our oft-undernourished psyches.

In a more playful light, as children we employ all the secret short-cuts to wishmaking that we possibly can. We shut our eyes and cross our little fingers when two of us utter the same word at the same exact instant; we "wish I may, wish I might," upon the first twinkling star in the heavens; and the grand daddy of all wishmakers—the wishbone—is a sought-after commodity when a meal features a tom or a hen.

Now is the time to get out your wish lists and heat up the stove. Though the little Y-bone delicacy is the charming spice of this soup, you may choose not to use it; a magical, unbreakable, large-enough-not-to-be-swallowed stone works well, too. To aid you, your kids, your friends, and beloved in reaching your dreams, I share my version of Wishing Soup. Feel free to refer to it for basic guidance and improvise to your liking—as with tastes, we all have different dreams, hopes, and wishes.

Wishing Soup

1 wishbone or large stone	1 tablespoon dried oregano
1 cup barley or orzo	1 tablespoon dried basil
1 tablespoon olive oil	Pinch of ginger (if your wish involves love)
1 onion, chopped	2 cups V-8 or tomato juice
1 red bell pepper, seeded and chopped	3 stalks celery, chopped
3 carrots, peeled and chopped or sliced	Half a head of cabbage, chopped (optional)
2 chicken or vegetable bouillon cubes	1 large tomato, chopped
2 tablespoons chopped fresh parsley	1 cup mushrooms, sliced
2 tablespoons dried thyme	Salt and pepper to taste

Light a yellow candle (for attraction), place your wishbone or rock next to it, close your eyes, and make your wish aloud.

In a medium saucepan, combine the barley or orzo with 4 cups water and bring to a boil; reduce heat and simmer until tender but not overcooked (8 to 10 minutes for orzo; 25 to 30 minutes for barley). Remove when done and set aside still in the cooking water.

While the barley or orzo is cooking, heat the oil in a large pot over medium heat. Add the onion, carrots, and bell pepper, and sauté for several minutes. Stir in 2 to 3 cups water (lesser measure if you prefer a thicker soup), the bouillon cubes, parsley, dried herbs, and ginger if you are using it. Bring mixture to a boil, then reduce heat to low.

Add the V-8 or tomato juice, celery, cabbage, and tomato. While stirring, drop the wishbone or stone in the soup, close your eyes, and whisper your wish. Simmer the soup over low heat for 15 to 20 minutes, until the vegetables are tender. Pour in the barley or orzo with its water. Stir in the mushrooms, and salt and pepper to taste. Cook for an additional 10 minutes.

Makes 1 great wish; serves 5 to 6 wishmakers.

A LA GODDESS

* Please take great care to remove the wishbone or stone before serving the soup. Set the wishbone aside to dry, cross your fingers, then snap it with a trustworthy friend. (Your wish is still *en force* even if you don't win the snap.) If you used a stone, toss it in a pond, stream, river, the sea, water fountain, or a lake to activate your wish.

If I were anyone else,
I'd envy me.

> —motto of Dorismarie Welcher,
> "Queen of the Hudson," septuagenarian

The Queen of the Hudson

Sometimes you meet a person of such grand humor, insight, integrity, and flair, you feel that they were sent into your life with a purpose and a gift. Such was my sensation upon meeting Dorismarie, Queen of the Hudson, who now rules the Hudson River from her vista in Manhattan. We literally met in the middle of nowhere—far from the Big Apple—out in a remote range of the Rocky Mountains in an area called Old Snowmass Valley about twenty miles from Aspen, Colorado. We were both solo; I was trying to find my way to a wedding and she was looking for someone fun to play with at the same wedding. Instant, albeit unlikely, soul mates, we have been friends ever since that day almost twenty years ago.

With guidance and zeal, she has brightened my life, made me laugh until I couldn't stand up, coached me through heartbreak and heartthrob (she once referred to an unsuitable suitor as "the Disneyland man"), and inspired me to unabashedly reach for the stars. Her entertaining way of seeing the world has taught me to laugh often, open my heart to the will of the universe, and expect miracles.

The first time I visited her home in Aspen, she was managing a household that included herself and four tenants, all late-teen to twenty-something young, unattached men whose only purpose was to party and ski. Now, imagine trying to get this entourage to clean the house. She would lament, "Margie, you can offer them sensual favors and hundred dollar bills, but you still can't get them to clean the windows." So, she devised a plan.

One Saturday morning, knowing they'd all come home hungry at noon, she fried up a batch of her famous chicken wings and I helped her bake a humongous batch of Cowboy Cookies. The Queen of the Hudson then displayed the bounty on comely plates on the dining room table, accompanied by fancy napkins and spotless beer glasses. She saw to it that energized rifts of great jazz wafted about the room along with the aromas of the meal. Then she elegantly and calmly took a seat at the table and waited.

When the guys came home, they instantly and eagerly dashed for the wings and cookies. When they reached for the prize, she stared at them with an eagle eye and in a breath-stopping voice said, "No, honey, not until you wash the windows, pick up your rooms, and take out the garbage." I've yet to see such a comical sight: four men who didn't know a dust bunny from a Playboy bunny, whirring around at the speed of sound, honoring her request in panting anticipation of wings, beer, and Cowboy Cookies. Beautiful. (Note that *sans* the beer, this tactic works equally well in luring recalcitrant kids to do their Saturday chores.)

I love eating these wings while luxuriating on a deck or porch by moonlight or lamplight. And with every bite, I can hear her laughter and see that mischievous sparkle in her eyes reflected in the night's sky.

The Queen's Wings

2 pounds plump chicken wings

Juice of one lemon

2 teaspoon black pepper,
coarsely ground

1½ teaspoon kosher salt

Paprika

Ground cayenne pepper

¾ cup flour

½ teaspoon ground turmeric (optional)

Canola or peanut oil for frying

Prepare the wings by removing and discarding the tips (they burn too quickly) and cutting them in half at the joint. Sprinkle the lemon juice over the wings and blanket with salt and black pepper. Season with paprika and a dash of cayenne pepper to suit your taste and set aside for 5 minutes.

Combine the flour, turmeric if using, and a few more dashes of cayenne in preferably a brown paper bag (a plastic bag will do). Shake together.

Cover the bottom of a heavy black iron skillet with a generous amount of oil and heat to hot, hot, hot, but not smoking (a drop of water should bounce off it) over medium-high heat.

Add 2 or 3 of the wing pieces at a time to the flour mixture in the bag and shake well, coating the pieces thoroughly. Shake off excess flour and arrange the wings in the skillet without crowding them; fry for 2 to 3 minutes, "skin side" down, until they are a crispy golden brown. (If all the wing pieces don't fit in your frying pan, either repeat the process or use dueling skillets.)

Turn the wings over, reduce the heat a notch, and cook, covered, for 6 to 8 more minutes. Remove the cover, poke at them and turn them a few more times to get them nice and crispy, and season with more salt, pepper and paprika if you desire.

Remove the wings from the skillet and set them on a brown paper bag or paper towels on the counter to help blot excess oil. Arrange them on a platter in an attractive "fan" design and serve with dip or alone.

Serves 2 to 4.

A la Goddess

* When the Queen has Lawry's Seasoned Salt on hand, she is known to replace the measure of salt and ground tumeric in the flour mixture with 2 teaspoons of Lawry's. Try it sometime for a little soul food flair.

———————————————⌁———————————————

Taking joy in life is a woman's best cosmetic.

—Rosalind Russell

It's Love with a Big Ladle

*M*y Irish friend Colleen was not born to cook (her contribution to ethnic potlucks is usually the Irish seven-course meal: a six-pack and a baked potato). She thought for years that a slice of heaven was being home alone with a book, a can of tuna, a bag of chips, and a glass of milk. Most times I've seen Col in the kitchen she is sitting on a high bar stool at the counter and sipping her coffee while devouring page after page of her latest book, she is not cooking.

But when her beloved grown-up kids celebrate their birthdays, it's always at Mom's house with Colleen's signature dish, her homemade chicken and nudes. (She has always playfully called her noodles "nudes.") This is a tummy-filling, high cholesterol, highly caloric, third-helping, plate-licking kind of dinner that assures your three-year old grandchild, your thirty-year-old child, and your lifetime lover that you love them most of all . . . and of course belies all that noncook nonsense of this particular chef. With Colleen, it's everlasting love with a big ladle. (Colleen's kitchen tip for making her Chicken and Nudes is to sing along with the "Ink Spots" record her Dad bought her in 1949.)

Colleen's Chicken and Nudes

1 boiling chicken (I remove the skin beforehand)	1 cup flour
1 can (14½ ounces) chicken broth	1 egg
Water with a pinch of salt	1 to 3 tablespoons milk
¼ teaspoon salt	Mashed potatoes (optional)

Place the cleaned chicken in a large pot and add broth and enough water to cover. Bring to a boil, then simmer for an hour or so until the poor chicken looks exhausted and ready to fall apart. Remove chicken and cool. Save broth.

Skin (if you haven't already) and bone the chicken, tearing or cutting the meat into bite-sized pieces. (At this point, Colleen salts and eats the heart and the gizzard. This is mainly so that, during the birthday dinner, no child in the family finds one of these critters swimming on his or her plate, and screams.)

Combine the flour and egg and add the milk, a tablespoon at a time, to form a very stiff dough. Mix thoroughly (with your hands if it's too stiff for a spoon). Roll out as thin as possible on a lightly floured pastry cloth—the dough should stretch to at least 15 or 16 inches in diameter.

Cut this dough in half, then slice the pieces into ½-inch-wide strips. Lay the strips, separated, on wax paper and let them dry on the counter. (Col often makes a double batch, as the offspring of this noncook love the nudes.) Bring broth to a low boil. Depending on your cooking schedule, the nudes can be tossed in the pot immediately—even if they are still slightly damp—or can lie around and dry all day. (You can also freeze them in a plastic bag for convenience sake.) Throw the chicken and nudes into the pot of broth, heat until nudes are cooked, and serve over mashed potatoes that have a dollop of butter on top.

Serves 6 children of any age.

Love is supreme and unconditional;
like is nice, but limited.

—Duke Ellington

We offer a prayer for peace and grace
and spiritual food,
For wisdom and guidance, for all these are good,
But don't forget the potatoes.

    —John Tyler Petter

How a Kitchen Goddess Spells H-o-m-e

*M*y variation of Mom's midwestern American version of meatloaf is inspired by a Slovenian version (thus the spelling of "musaka") probably derived from a German adaptation of a Hungarian version of a greatly modified Greek version of moussaka, a layered dish of eggplant, ground meat— probably lamb—and white sauce. Oh how fun to be a Kitchen Goddess!

I always serve it topped with my special mashed potatoes, made with mayonnaise. By the way, the name "mayonnaise"—the secret ingredient in all my mashed potatoes—is derived from the Minorcan seaport town of Port Mahon where it is said to have originated. And the Fates have rendered us fortunate enough here in the colonies to readily possess the "secret sauce"—Heinz ketchup—that ties the taste up with a big, blue ribbon.

Meatloaf Musaka

1½ pounds ground chuck or sirloin

1 onion, finely chopped

¼ cup finely chopped fresh parsley sprig

2 or 3 cloves garlic, minced

1 egg

1 cup quick-cooking oats, uncooked

¼ cup sweet relish (Claussen's is best)

½ cup Heinz ketchup

2 teaspoons dry leaf oregano

1 teaspoon paprika

1 teaspoon salt

¼ teaspoon ground cinnamon

1 teaspoon curry (optional)

1 tablespoon brown sugar

1 tablespoon Tabasco sauce or additional ketchup

1 teaspoon cayenne pepper (optional)

¼ cup grated fresh Parmesan cheese

Musaka Mashed Potatoes (recipe follows)

Preheat oven to 350°F. In a large bowl, combine all ingredients, except additional ketchup, brown sugar, mashed potatoes, and Parmesan thoroughly (I just use clean hands and goosh it up.) Grease a 9-by-5-inch loaf pan or a 2-quart round casserole dish and fill with meat mixture. Cover the top with additional ketchup and the brown sugar. Top with a shake of salt and pepper and bake uncovered for 1 hour.

While the meat is cooking, boil and mash potatoes. After 1 hour, pull the meatloaf from the oven and increase the temperature to 400°F. Cover the meatloaf with approximately 1 inch of mashed potatoes, adorn with Parmesan, and bake 5 to 7 more minutes until cheese melts.

Serves 6.

Musaka Mashed Potatoes

3 large potatoes, peeled and cut

1 tablespoon butter

2 tablespoons mayonnaise, any kind

¼ cup warm milk, 1 tablespoon at a time

Salt, pepper, garlic powder, and paprika to taste

Place the potatoes in a large saucepan, cover with water, and bring to a boil over high heat. Reduce heat and place a lid askew on the pan to allow steam to escape and help prevent a potato-water eruption. Cook for about 20 minutes until potatoes are tender.

Drain the water and return pan to the stove top, heat off. (The remaining heat will steam out excess moisture and reduce starchiness.) Begin mashing the potatoes, together with the butter and mayonnaise. Slowly add warm milk, 1 teaspoon at a time, until you've reached the right texture. Season to taste with salt, pepper, garlic powder, and paprika, and beat until creamy and fluffy.

A la Goddess

* For an extra kick and a wild taste, try lacing the oats with 2½ tablespoons bourbon before adding them to the meat. When I incite this flavor fest, I usually also toss in 2 tablespoons brown sugar to enhance the excitement. Fear not, it is absolutely fun and flavorful and will keep the taste buds in awe. Also, if you are inflicted with an aversion to ketchup, simply use tomato sauce—canned or fresh—in its place and add 1 teaspoon vinegar, 1 tablespoon brown sugar, and 1 more tablespoon quick-cooking oats.

The Best Is Baked to Be

With the advent of the bread machine, there was a widespread, albeit technical, renaissance of baking yeast breads. Though I wholeheartedly support this marvelous shortcut to transcending the indignities of plastic-wrapped, grocery-bought "balloon breads," I challenge you to get your hands and soul into some dynamite dough and knead up the real thing. Many a meal can be sanctified with a warm loaf of hand-shaped, homebaked bread.

With all bread-baking deities out there who accept this summons (yeast breads have been with us for nearly four thousand years), I share the most sacred secret words in the glutinous galaxy: SAF-Instant yeast. With this magic, high-performance, highly porous yeast, developed in France, bread will rise in approximately half the time. You can add the yeast directly to the flour without having to dissolve it, and it produces consistent loaves, impressive in both texture and taste. If you can't find it about town, call the King Arthur Baking Company at 800-827-6836 or go online at www.kingarthurflour.com to order it.

Love cures people—both the ones who give it,
and the ones who receive it.

—Dr. Karl Menninger

Where Intention Goes, Energy Flows

*D*irectly linked with the earth-mother goddess and worshipped as the "staff of life," bread has been a divine substance, literally and figuratively, for more than eight thousand years. Consequently, symbolism, lore, and ritual are deeply kneaded into this great food. Sacrificial loaves were offered to appease the ancient deities and magical powers were ascribed to those who carried a morsel of bread with them—protection, avoidance of danger and theft, blessings of abundance. In Biblical lore, *manna* floated from the heavens to nourish the people of the desert, and Jesus Christ forever sacralized the "heavenly host" when he broke bread and passed it around at the Last Supper.

The legend that goes with this recipe for Olympic Squaw Bread, acquired when I was baking professionally near Olympic Valley, in California, is told by Native American Washoe women preparing a revered and life-sustaining bread using ingredients indigenous to the area.

I recommend your making the full recipe of this exquisite and teasingly sweet staple, therefore budgeting future time for other pleasures: Whether you are making one loaf or four, the bread will essentially take the same time to prepare. I promise you, this bread makes a supreme potluck or gift offering, and it freezes like a charm. For cheese-and-bread, a dinner bread, a sandwich bread, or a hearty French toast breakfast bread, Olympic Squaw Bread is indubitably upper crust!

The ritual of baking yeast breads provides a grounding time for what I call the *motion meditation*. While kneading the dough, let your mind slip away to that cool, clear paradise of free-flowing, delicious, light thought. If your mind jumps track to mundane concerns, simply stop kneading the bread, take a deep breath, blink ten times, and begin again. Remember: Where intention goes, energy flows.

Olympic Squaw Bread

2 cups warm water

1½ cups brown sugar

2 tablespoons SAF-Instant dry baker's yeast

¼ cup canola oil

2 tablespoons buttermilk or milk

2 teaspoons salt

1 large egg

4 cups whole wheat flour

8 cups unbleached flour

2 cups shredded apples

1 cup chopped walnuts

Canola oil for greasing

Cornmeal

Pour the water into a very large (at least 13-quart) bowl and add the sugar but do not mix. Sprinkle the yeast on top of the sugar water and set aside for 5 minutes. Then, add oil, buttermilk or milk, salt, egg, whole wheat flour, 4 cups of the unbleached white flour, apples, and walnuts. Mix with a *very* sturdy mixing spoon. Gradually add the remaining flour until you've achieved the right texture—the dough should feel warm and smooth like your cheeks when you smile. (The exact amount of flour you use will depend on its moisture content and the humidity level of your kitchen.) Knead the dough for about 5 minutes. Lightly oil the dough and return it to a greased bowl. Cover with a clean damp cloth and set in a warm place.

When the dough has doubled in size—30 minutes or more depending on where you live—punch it down and knead it again for about 5 minutes. Divide the dough and shape it into 3 rounds. Place on a cookie sheet that is sprinkled with cornmeal or lined with parchment. Slash the top surface of the loaves twice with a sharp knife, and let rise another 30 minutes or so, until almost doubled.

Bake in a preheated oven at 375°F for 15 minutes, then reduce heat to 350°F and bake for another 20 to 25 minutes, or until the loaves sound hollow when tapped. When hot out of the oven, the loaves can be brushed with melted butter to activate the magic.

Makes three 1-pound loaves.

Why has our poetry eschewed
The rapture and response of food?
What hymns are sung,
What praises said
For homemade miracles of bread?

—Louis Untermeyer

The energy of the creative impulse comes from love and all its manifestations—admiration, compassion, glowing respect, gratitude, praise, tenderness, adoration, enthusiasm—and remember the word 'enthusiasm' means 'divine inspiration.'

—Brenda Ueland, *If You Want to Write*

A Sure-Fire Offering

The fire goddess Pele holds court on the island of Hawaii. She is a smoldering and explosive soul, and many fear her, for good reason. Pele's realm is one of the most active volcanos in the world, Kilauea. Locals believe that it is important to appease her with prayers and offerings, so that she will leave the islands undisturbed.

When making this colorful, aromatic sweet loaf, the motion meditation of kneading usually whisks me to a warm, embracing, sandy beach on a subtropical island. The sun feels like a big, toasty hug from mom, and a slight wind caresses my ankles. Mountains of fresh mangoes, papayas, and pineapple are mine for the picking, and happy thoughts hopscotch through my mind. And in this fun-shine daydream, I always have a loaf of sweet potato bread—one of the most flavorful breads I have tasted—to share with the goddess Pele.

Hawaiian Sweet Potato Bread

2 large sweet potatoes

5 teaspoons SAF-Instant dry baker's yeast
or 2 packages (7 grams) active dry yeast

1¼ cups lukewarm water

¼ cup brown or raw sugar

¾ cup milk or oat milk (available in the
natural food section of most supermarkets)

2 teaspoons salt

¼ cup canola oil

1 egg

2 cups whole wheat flour

4 to 5 cups unbleached white flour

Cream of Wheat cereal or cornmeal

Bake the sweet potatoes for about an hour in a 350°F oven. When they are cooked, peel and mash them—you should have about 1½ cups mashed potatoes.

In a large bread bowl, dissolve the yeast in ¼ cup lukewarm water. After a few minutes, stir in the mashed sweet potatoes, sugar, remaining cup of water, milk, salt, oil, and egg. Mix in whole wheat flour and half of the unbleached white flour with a *very* sturdy mixing spoon. Gradually add the remaining flour until the dough has the right texture. It should feel warm and smooth, not sticky. Remember, the exact amount of flour you need depends on the humidity of the kitchen and the moisture content of the flour.

Knead the dough for about 7 minutes until elastic. Place it in a greased bowl, and lightly oil the top. Cover with a towel and set in a warm place until doubled in size—(25 to 30 minutes with SAF-Instant yeast; almost twice that time for active dry yeast; see yeast information on page 35).

Dough is ready if, when you touch it, a finger impression remains. Punch it down, divide it in half, and knead again for about 5 minutes. Form into baguettes and place them on a parchment-lined cookie sheet dusted with Cream of Wheat or cornmeal. (If you prefer using a loaf pan to bake your bread, do it!) Lightly slash the tops of the loaves in several spots with a very sharp knife. Cover again, and let loaves rise another 25 minutes or so, until almost doubled.

Bake in a preheated oven at 325°F for 50 minutes to an hour, or until done (loaves will sound hollow if you tap them). When the loaves emerge hot out of the oven, brush the tops with melted butter.

Makes two 12- to 18-inch baguettes.

A la Goddess

* For fancy occasions, I braid the dough. To do this, divide dough into 6 portions after the first rising. Shape the dough into long rolls, and, for each loaf, braid 3 of them, tucking the ends under the loaf. Because there is more mass to the loaves, they may Take longer to bake.

  Makes 2 stocky, braided loaves.

To be simple is to be great.

—Emerson

A contented heart makes all food good.

—Venice J. Bloodworth

Mom's Magic Mixing Bowl

*T*he first time I realized that my own mother had magical powers in the kitchen was upon licking the batter-coated spoon that she had used to mix her banana bread. This recipe works best if done by hand, and not with an electric mixer. Perhaps it's all the love stirred in by hand that makes it so good. Simply and shamelessly stated, I proclaim this to be the best recipe of its kind in the modern baking world . . . bet on it.

Bella Banana Bread

4 cups unbleached white flour

2 cups brown sugar

I teaspoon salt

I teaspoon baking soda

4 eggs

2 teaspoons pure vanilla extract

⅔ cup buttermilk

I cup canola oil or melted margarine

4 large, *very ripe*, mashed bananas

2 cups chopped nuts—walnuts, pecans, or
    any nut you love (optional)

Additional brown sugar and nuts (optional)

Preheat oven to 350°F. Grease two 8-by-4-inch loaf pans. (Heart-shaped baking pans add a special touch; you can also use muffin tins.) Combine the flour, sugar, salt, and baking soda in a large bowl. Make a well in the center.

In a separate bowl, whisk the eggs, vanilla, and buttermilk together. Pour into the well and mix slightly. Add oil and mix a bit. Last, add the mashed bananas and nuts, if using. Mix together delicately, taking care not to overmix.

Spoon batter into the prepared pans and sprinkle the tops with additional brown sugar and/or nuts, if desired.

Bake for 45 to 55 minutes; check for doneness by inserting a wooden toothpick in the center of the loaf or by pushing the top with your finger. If the toothpick comes out clean or if the bread springs back, it's done. If you use other pans, baking time will vary of course. (I prefer to underbake rather than overbake; this insures the bread will freeze well.)

Makes 2 loaves or 14 standard muffins or a dozen jumbo muffins.

A la Goddess

* To make this recipe a bit more angelic, I would suggest any or all of the following:
    Replace the eggs with 1 egg plus 4 egg whites
    Reduce the sugar to 1½ cup, and use 1 cup plus 2 tablespoons of unsweetened applesauce instead of oil
    Omit the nuts and/or the topping

* If you don't have buttermilk on hand, use ⅔ cup milk plus 1 tablespoon vinegar. Or use yogurt (any flavor is fine) in place of the buttermilk and add 2 tablespoons milk.

* Add 1 cup of frozen blueberries and/or peach slices or pineapple chunks—fruit really enhances the flavor and surprise factor of Bella Banana Bread. Try it!

Monkey See—Monkey Eat

Kids just adore the name of this fun-to-eat, sweet, sticky, pull-apart biscuit: monkey bread. Though I have yet to unearth its true etymology (every opinion of the origin seems to differ), the closest congruency I've found is that it resembles the fruit of the African baobab tree and that we probably look like monkeys when we eat it—pulling it apart, piece by gooey, glorious piece—and grabbing it from other monkeys at the table.

I've decided that monkey bread leans toward being more of a concept than a word: *monkey around, monkey with, monkey-faced, monkey hunt, monkey business, monkey shine, monkey-see monkey-do, make a monkey out of eating monkey bread!* You *do* monkey bread. If there were an award for "the food most fun to play with," Piña Colada Monkey Bread would swing away with the prize.

Piña Colada Monkey Bread

½ cup fresh coconut

½ cup butter

½ cup brown sugar

2 teaspoons ground cinnamon

½ teaspoon ground nutmeg

½ cup crushed pineapple in natural juices

1 tablespoon rum (optional)

½ cup white sugar

¼ cup brown sugar

½ cup chopped macadamia nuts (optional)

4 tubes of Pillsbury buttermilk biscuits (7.5-ounces each)

Pierce the coconut and drain milk. Reserve. Crack the coconut and scrape the flesh from the sides. Shred the coconut flesh and mix ½ cup with the reserved milk to form a mulch.

In a large heavy saucepan, melt butter, brown sugar, ½ teaspoon of the cinnamon, and the nutmeg over medium-low heat. When mixture starts to bubble, add the crushed pineapple, coconut mixture, and optional rum. Cook until bubbling (5 to 10 minutes), taking care not to burn, and remove from heat.

Cut each biscuit into quarters. Combine white and brown sugar and remaining 1½ teaspoons cinnamon in a medium-sized brown paper bag or large plastic container with a lid. Taking a handful of biscuits at a time, shake them in the bag or container until each portion of dough is well dusted with sugar. Set biscuits aside.

Preheat oven to 350°F. Grease and flour a Bundt pan. Sprinkle chopped macadamia nuts and any leftover cinnamon-sugar in the bottom of the pan. Place half of the biscuits in the pan, and pour half the syrup mixture over them. Arrange the remaining biscuits in the pan and pour the remaining syrup over them. Bake for 35 to 40 minutes. Invert Bundt pan onto a plate and serve sticky and hot.

Serves 6 to 8.

A LA GODDESS

* If you are not cuckoo for coconut and don't want the challenge or the hassle of cracking the beast:

    Replace the coconut mixture with ⅓ cup Coco Casa Cream of Coconut or ⅓ cup evaporated milk plus 1 teaspoon vanilla or coconut extract; or

    Soak ⅓ cup dry, flaked coconut for about five minutes in enough milk to make ½ cup.

The pursuit of perfection, then,
is the pursuit of sweetness and light.

—Matthew Arnold

Hand-Held Happiness

*T*he easiest way to bring happiness to the world is to make a batch of these goodies and practice inspired "random acts of kindness" by giving them away to strangers. I discovered this original hand-written recipe when shuffling through a friend's mother's 1950s cookbook. Today, perhaps because cereal companies want you to use more cereal and so many worried souls are all worked up about fat content, the recipe on the Rice Krispies box calls for six cups of cereal and less butter. But I prefer the old-time, chewier, richer version. Whichever way you crisp 'em, they instantly find that happy note in the heart the moment they tickle the taste buds. Here's to the most wonderful memories of childhood!

Rice Crispee Cakes

¼ cup margarine

1 package (10 ounces) of large marshmallows or 4 cups minimarshmallows

½ teaspoon ground cinammon (optional)

5 cups crispy rice cereal

Before you do anything, choose your pans and lubricate them. A 13-by-9-by-2-inch pan is standard for this recipe, but feel free to be creative. I often line up open-top cookie cutters or tuna cans with tops and bottoms removed on a cookie sheet lined with waxed paper—muffin-top tins also make great individual "rice cakes."

In a large saucepan, melt the margarine over very low heat. Add the marshmallows and stir until melted. Stir in the optional cinnamon and remove from heat. Add the rice cereal and stir until coated. Press the glorious, golden, gooey mixture into place with waxed paper or a buttered object such as a spoon or a spatula or the heel of your hand.

Makes twenty-four 2-by-2-inch squares if made in the standard pan.

A la Goddess

* The variations to this winning recipe seem endless. Let's see, what can we do to jazz it up today?

> Add 1 cup M&Ms or Hershey's Mini-Kisses
> Add 1 cup rum-soaked raisins
> Add 1 cup pistachios
> Stir ¼ cup almond butter into marshmallow mixture before adding cereal
> Shape them into balls
> Roll the balls in melted chocolate
> Make them with Cocoa Krispies-type cereal
> Add 1 cup butterscotch chips
> Use food coloring to make them blue ... or purple ... or ....
>
> Let's pause here. Let your imagination take flight back into your childhood, and

mix the Rice Crispee Cakes exactly the way you always wanted Mom to make them. No moms are watching over our shoulders now, so eat as many as you want and share with whomever you please!

A Kitchen Nymph in an Apron Told Me

To avoid those petty and pesky technical difficulties when baking, photocopy this checklist and tape it front-and-center in your kitchen.

* Use an audible timer (the necklace-type is particularly effective)
* Use an oven thermometer until you know your oven
* Always set your timer a few minutes before the prescribed "done" time; to check for doneness, resort to the old-fashioned touch test (the top should spring back when touched; or, bread should sound hollow when thumped) or use a toothpick
* Open and shut oven doors slowly, as if you are moving in slow motion
* Grease and flour pans well to prevent sticking—Baker's Joy (aerosol cooking spray) is the best for this
* Use baking parchment paper (bribe the counter person at your local supermarket bakery for the big sheets)
* Unless otherwise specified, work with room-temperature ingredients—avoid extremes

In other words, stay aware and don't get caught with your apron up around your eyes.

To Each His Cookie

I have discovered that every man has a favorite cookie. Not an "Oh, this is a tasty cookie" preference, but rather a more direct "If you're going to bake me cookies, don't waste your time on anything but *this* cookie" attitude. With the exception of one person I know (who is addicted to my Chocolate Chip Classics but had never tasted a chocolate chip cookie—or peanut butter and jelly sammies—until he was almost finished with college), most of these long-standing cookie love affairs began in childhood. In all probability, Mom baked a special batch *just for him* (Goddesses, remember; "Once an accident, twice a habit"), and it forever imprinted that magical quality of feeling like a prince.

'Tis true: I can tell you the pet cookie of almost every man I know. It's a fun hobby. It seems to me that women, though certainly able to declare their choicest desserts, aren't as emotionally attached to cookies as men. Please indulge me in my thesis— explore for yourselves!

Cookies, from *koekje*, the Dutch diminutive of "cake," have been baked for ritual and divination purposes for centuries. The pagan practice of symbolically shaping the cookies into circles (the sun), stars (protection from negative forces), trees (fertility), and bells (to drive away evil) has nestled itself comfortably in the custom of Yule baking; small gingerbreadlike hard cakes were also offered as sacrifices to the goddesses and gods at this time of year. An ancient Roman practice called *aleuromancy* involved the random distribution of cakes that were impregnated with messages and fortunes written on paper. Today we call them "fortune cookies." (Maybe the guys are onto something . . . cookies do seem to hold an incomparable mystique found in few edible treats.)

The chewy, moist, perfectly sweet confection made from the recipe below claims the honor of being the ultimate cookie dough recipe to be used in Cookie Dough Pancakes (page 15). Years ago, I regularly sent my friend, Lyon Polk, who now lives in New York City with his daughters and wife, tins of these cookies to keep him inspired on several projects. When he first married, I bestowed my original recipe upon him and his new bride; I wonder if they are still his favorites.

Royal Oatmeal Raisin Cookies

1½ cups (12 ounces) margarine, at room temperature

2 cups brown sugar

1 cup white sugar

2 large eggs

2 teaspoons pure vanilla extract

½ cup water

1 teaspoon salt

¾ teaspoon ground cinnamon (optional)

1 teaspoon baking soda

2¼ cups unbleached white flour

6 cups old-fashioned oats

2 cups golden raisins or sultanas (if you're fortunate enough to find them)

In a large mixing bowl, whip up the margarine and sugars until fluffy. Add the eggs, vanilla, water, salt, and cinnamon if desired, and mix well.

Blend the baking soda into the flour, either directly in the measuring cup or in a medium bowl, and tap it into the wet ingredients, stirring slowly. Stir in the oats and raisins by hand. Cover the bowl and let dough rest for 15 to 20 minutes. This allows the oats to absorb moisture, which is essential to the success of a perfect cookie.

Preheat the oven to 350°F. Line a cookie sheet with baking parchment and scoop the dough with a small ice cream scoop. Bake for 10 to 12 minutes until

golden brown. Note your baking time for next time.
Makes forty 2-ounce cookies.

A LA GODDESS

* The dough keeps refrigerated for about two days; set some aside in case you want to
use it for Cookie Dough Pancakes.

**Nothing is much sweeter
than the sincere gratification—
and admiration—of a friend.**

—Anonymous

The secret to making good bread is that there is no secret.
Let your imagination help you break any rules
you imagine exist to daunt you.

—Jacqueline Deval, *Reckless Appetites*

A Friend's Sweet Advice

I'll refrain from mentioning names, but a now-cooled flame of mine once called these his favorites. Given to me by Simone, my friend and once-upon-a-time cookie shop partner, the original recipe called for even more peanut butter. Go ahead—up the peanut butter to two cups if you're a peanut butter cookie fanatic. As Simone said, "Margie, you can never have too much fun or too much peanut butter."

Peanut Butter Crisscross Cookies

1 cup margarine, at room temperature	¼ teaspoon salt
1 cup white sugar	1¾ cups peanut butter, chunky or smooth
1 cup brown sugar	1 teaspoon baking soda
3 eggs	3 cups unbleached white flour
1 teaspoon pure vanilla extract	

Preheat oven to 350°F. In a large mixing bowl, beat the margarine and sugars until fluffy. Add the eggs, vanilla, and salt and mix well. Gently mix in the peanut butter.

Blend the baking soda into the flour, either directly in the measuring cup or in a bowl, and tap flour into the creamed mixture, stirring slowly until well blended.

With a small ice cream scoop, scoop out 1- to 2-ounce balls of dough onto a parchment-lined cookie sheet. With a 4-tined fork, press the top of the cookie gently to make a classic crisscross design. Bake for 8 to 10 minutes until golden. Take a bite and zoom directly back to your childhood.

Makes approximately twenty-five 2-ounce cookies.

A LA GODDESS

* Another famously popular modification of this recipe is the Peanut Butter Chocolate Chip Cookie; simply toss in a cup of chocolate chips. A kitchen goddess I know suggests another tasty variation, the Peanut Butter Raisin Crisscross, made by adding 1 cup of raisins to the recipe. Enjoy!

You Teach What You Need to Learn

*T*ommy, a young man who attended one of my high-altitude baking classes at Sierra Nevada College, waltzed into class with these unbelievably great ginger cookies. His grandmother had taught him how to make them. I was so impressed when I bit into one; and I am so touched that Tommy was willing to share this recipe with me.

Tommy's Gingers

¾ cup margarine, at room temperature`

½ cup white sugar

½ cup brown sugar, unpacked

¼ cup molasses

I egg

I tablespoon ground ginger

2 teaspoons ground cinnamon

2 cups unbleached white flour

½ teaspoon salt

2 teaspoons baking soda

Extra white sugar

Preheat oven to 400°F. In a large bowl, cream the margarine and sugars together until fluffy. Add the molasses, egg, ginger, and cinnamon and beat well.

Combine the flour, salt, and baking soda and gently add to the creamed ingredients. Shape dough into 1-inch balls by rolling gingerly in the palm of your hands. Roll the balls in sugar, place on a parchment-lined baking sheet, press slightly, and bake for 6 to 8 minutes. If you prefer them chewier, bake at 350°F for 8 to 10 minutes.

Makes approximately 20 cookies.

The Enchantress
of All Cookies

When scientists immortalized chocolate with the name *theobroma cacao*, which means food of the gods, they must have been dreaming of this very cookie. The Ultimate Chocolate Chip Classics—the unrivalled, bestselling two-ounce cookie in my bakery—and my trademarked creation, the quarter-pound Cowboy Cookie, acquired a zealously devoted following at Margie's Cowboy Cookies. I, as the conjurer of the cookies, became something of a local baking legend. People honestly *believed* that my creations possessed special powers, and I playfully accepted my unofficial title as the kitchen goddess.

One cookie connoisseur and demigod I know confided, "I've never met a better set of chocolate chips—even on Mrs. Fields' trays." Chips up, these are about the best you can scoop. They keep nicely in tins or ziplock plastic bags, and freeze well for up to a week. The uncooked dough also freezes well for four to five days.

Margie's Ultimate Chocolate Chip Classics

½ cup margarine at room temperature

½ cup butter at room temperature

1 cup brown sugar

1 cup white sugar

2 eggs

1 teaspoon pure vanilla extract

½ teaspoon salt

1 teaspoon baking soda

1 teaspoon baking powder

3 cups unbleached white flour

2 cups chocolate chips

Preheat the oven to 350°F. In a large (at least 13-quart) mixing bowl, and using an electric mixer, whip up margarine, butter, and sugars until fluffy. Add the eggs, vanilla, and salt and mix well.

Blend the baking soda, baking powder, and flour, either directly in the measuring cup (my preferred method) or in a large bowl, and tap into the creamed mixture, beating on low speed. With a strong wooden spoon, stir in the chocolate chips.

Line a cookie sheet with baking parchment and scoop the dough with a small (1- to 2-ounce) ice cream scoop. Press the top of the cookie dough mound down oh-so-slightly. Cast your spell over the first tray of chippers and bake for 9 to 11 minutes, until lightly golden in color with tiny cracks on top of the cookies. Note your baking time for the rest of the batch.

Makes about two dozen 2-ounce Mrs. Fields'-size cookies.

A LA GODDESS

* If you're aiming for an even more delicate, melt-in-your-mouth-but-crunchy crust and an ecstatically gooey inside, substitute 1¼ cups oat flour for 1 cup of the unbleached white flour in the recipe.

* Yes, there is a secret to this recipe: the chocolate chips. My favorite baking chips are, have been, and always will be Hershey's. (Sorry, Nestlé, but your Toll House biscuits never matched my vision of a perfect chocolate chip cookie.) The advice continues (drum roll here . . .): I *always* use half semisweet and half milk chocolate. On festive occasions, try tossing in white chocolate chips, a few toffee chips, or Mini-Kisses.

* For an enchanted touch, press some of the dough into a greased and parchment-lined heart-shaped pan. Bake for 17 to 20 minutes or until golden brown. After the cookie has cooled, write a special message on top or frost with your favorite frosting.

Time and Time Again

I think sometimes that Einstein's ghost haunts my kitchen; perhaps he just likes the relative taste of my cookies. You see, time is not linear in the goddess' kitchen. Every single time I cook something, it takes a different time to cook. A barrage of variables lurks in even the dandiest of culinary laboratories: low- and high-pressure systems being ushered in with seasonal winds; temperature tangos between sunlit days and moonlit nights; different textures of butters, flours, and sugars from brand to brand; and an occasional prank-loving poltergeist, as there is with my kitchen.

Be conscious of your *time* when you bake or cook, and always note the closest linear *time* to cooking perfection on the recipe for the future. Don't trust the *time* given on any recipe until you've experimented on your own. Set a *timer*. With one of those stylish necklace *timers* from Germany, you can even go do a little yoga in between cookie batches. And don't forget to take your *time*—enjoying the process is what transforms cooking into pleasure.

Food of the Goddess

On the day my beloved mentor and friend Dorismarie decided to leave Aspen and take up residence in New York City, she handed me a piece of paper with a cookie recipe scribbled on it and said, "Here Margie, take this. Knowing your ingenious Aquarian mind, you'll discover a way to make a lot of money with this someday." And millions I made . . . cookies, however, not dollars, and some of the best friends and fondest memories of my life.

During my rookie season managing bakeries at the Squaw Valley USA ski area in the Sierra Nevada, it rained on Christmas. Then a drought year ensued, and with it a desperate lack of skiers. The livelihoods of my hired bakers were at stake. Faced with what seemed to be the inevitable—having to fire these people because there was no work for them—I went to a beach at Lake Tahoe to make angels in the sand and hope for an epiphany. The next day while I was riding on the chairlift, the "A-ha!" hit me: Dig out that Cowboy Cookie recipe from Dorismarie and begin baking and selling them at the mountain.

By taking the chance at a spin with the Cowboy Cookies, we hit our number at job-security roulette that ski season. Sales increased, and my simple objective of preserving the jobs of my baking crew was fulfilled. That spring, I talked my employer into leasing the kitchen to me after hours so I could produce cookies for a moonlighting wholesale business. The following year, 1986, I opened a retail outlet in Tahoe City, California, with Simone Gerstner, friend and cookie fan; with a plate of hot cookies, we had persuaded another friend, Bob Rudy, to finance the dream. Margie's Cowboy Cookies was in the chips.

The Cowboy Cookies charmed my life in so many ways. With a tin of cookies in hand, I developed enduring friendships. I traded cookies for skis, for backstage concert passes (thank you, Eileen and Cassidy), for hotel accommodations, for fun. I convinced a car dealer to let me drive away in a new car with no money down and no credit history. I baked them for my husband-to-be on one of our first dates, undoubtedly a catalyst in sealing our fate.

Through the cookie connection, I developed the will and experience to nurture a dream—simply stated, it is because of the Cowboy Cookies that we are together at this moment on this page as I write and you read. The mystical and powerful connection between sharing special foods and creating a life of pride and pleasure, and vice versa, became crystal clear to me . . . and I'm encouraging you to explore it, too.

This is, most unquestionably, my favorite recipe—the ultimate, unsurpassed, spellbinding love-and-fun potion! With a batch of these gems in hand, expect serendipitous, magic-carpet, Cowboy Cookie adventures to fly into your life. So, lighten up and ride 'em, cowgirls!

Margie's Cowboy Cookies

1½ cups margarine at room temperature

2 cups brown sugar

2 cups white sugar

4 eggs

2 teaspoons pure vanilla extract

1 teaspoon salt

1 teaspoon baking powder

2 teaspoons baking soda

4 cups unbleached white flour

4 cups old-fashioned oats

2 cups Hershey's chocolate chips

1 cup coconut

1 cup chopped nuts

Preheat oven to 350°F. With an electric mixer, whip up the margarine and sugars in a large mixing bowl until fluffy. Add the eggs, vanilla, and salt and beat well.

Blend the baking soda and baking powder into the flour, either directly in the measuring cup or in a large bowl, and then tap this mixture into the creamed ingredients, mixing slowly. Now, grab a sturdy wooden spoon and do the rest by hand. Add your oats and stir until the dough comes together. Last, stir in chocolate chips, coconut, and nuts.

Line a cookie sheet with baking parchment (the secret to perfectly baked cookies!) and scoop the dough with a 2-ounce ice cream scoop. Press the top of the cookie dough mound down oh-so-slightly. Cast your spell over the Cowboy Cookies and bake for 7 to 12 minutes, until lightly golden in color with tiny cracks on top of the cookies.

Makes approximately four dozen 2-ounce cookies.

Cookie of Childhood

The best recipes in life are sometimes hidden in books that rarely make it to a cook's shelf. Such are the savors in *Peace Is Every Step* by Thich Nhat Hanh, a nominee for the Nobel Peace prize and an unassuming connoisseur of the flavors of life. In his book he reminds us, "Eating mindfully is a most important practice . . . we can eat in a way that we restore the cookie of our childhood. The present moment is filled with joy and happiness. If you are attentive, you will see it."

My favorite entry is "Aimlessness," about which he says, "There is a word in Buddhism that means 'wishlessness' or 'aimlessness.' The idea is that you do not put something in front of you and run after it, because everything is already here, in yourself . . . Whether we are eating a tangerine, drinking a cup of tea, or walking in meditation, we should do it in a way that is 'aimless.'"

Right on target, Thich, right on target.

We must empower
our wealth with wisdom,
our power with purpose,
our grace with beauty.

—John F. Kennedy

CHAPTER 3

In Aphrodite's Mixing Bowl

Delicious Pleasures
AND
Tasty Favorites

Considered solely in connection with pleasures of the table,
a wanton woman is one who with cunning and deliberation
prepares a meal which will draw another person to her.

—M. F. K. Fisher

The Goddess of Love was a very busy girl: She bore more children than any other goddess—at least one or two, by some accounts three, from each of her liaisons with numerous gods and unsuspecting mortal men. Though she probably didn't possess the time or inclination to occupy her days with cooking, she was well versed in how to harness alchemical powers to be released at well-planned feasts that were set forth with flirtatious flair. When coaching women who called on her for lessons in playful seduction, Aphrodite assuredly stirred it up with playful passion, enchantment, and satisfaction in mind.

There is much to learn from this energetic goddess about loving, romance, and cooking and how to blend these ingredients masterfully and effortlessly together in a fast-forward, sometimes challenging world of relationships. The great Aphrodite would certainly counsel her eager courtiers to focus on love and fun and keep the cooking simple. With her lively spirit to guide us, we would realize that a kitchen goddess does not *have* to cook to seduce—simply being in the kitchen engaged in a nurturing act of love is a seduction in itself. In order to keep passions fresh and flowing, Aphrodite would undoubtedly swear by the Kitchen Goddess Manifesto #1: Do not cook if you are in a bad mood, lack the desire, or feel pressure from the nagging obligation to another.

Spontaneity and genuine desire would be her foremost spices. Breakfast, with its languid introduction to a crisp new day, would probably be her favorite meal to prepare. My notion is that her definitive word of wisdom would be *atmosphere*. A goddess in the kitchen would know to keep as her staples candles, flowers, mood-setting music, and incense, if desired, along with favorite feel-good foods and special concoctions such as Champagne and hot chocolate. Most of all, she would know how to keep the mystery and the magic stirring right along with her soups and her mixing spoons.

The purpose of a cookery book is unmistakable.
Its object can conceivably be no other
than to increase the happiness of mankind.

—Joseph Conrad

I loved him, or thought I loved him,
which is the same thing.

—Coco Chanel

Not-Quite-So Politically Correct Advice
from a Kitchen Goddess

*T*he quest for love has led too many women down devious and disappointing paths. Far too often, in a desperate search for Cupid's arrow, women have futilely exhausted their energy and resources: Riches have been dissipated on insanely expensive cosmetics in vain attempts to hide sad smiles or on hair colorings in hopes of masking heads full of misgivings; time has been misspent on reading addicting romance novels and magazine articles with ridiculous titles like "How to Win His Love by Dating His Best Friend." Thoughts that could have been channeled into creative and inspired action have been squandered on obsessive imaginings about "Mr. Fantasy."

Dear ladies and goddesses, please listen. Let me reveal a priceless, timeless secret. The wisest investment you will ever make in attracting and securing a loving man is a simple, yet powerfully intoxicating tool: a cookbook—a collection of love potions.

* *"Woo with food as well as flattery."*

* *"Kissin' don't last—cookin' do!"*

* *"The way to a man's heart is . . . ."*

Believe this ancient wisdom. Just as the artist creates a masterpiece with canvas and brush, so an artful kitchen goddess with her cookbook and sensuous imagination creates a satisfied and attentive companion. The art of seduction can be mastered simply by learning to concoct spellbinding foods, and knowing when and how to serve them forth.

Vital information, such as a detailed account of your potential squire's soul-stirring favorite foods must be oh-so-subtly extracted from him when you first meet—his dearest dessert, the beloved things mom used to cook for him, and his ideas of mouth-watering meals and libations. Then consult your book of wisdom and find the irresistible variations of those endearments.

A man's needs for nourishment and love are so intricately interwoven that often he makes no distinction between the two. As you prepare a tantalizing Garden of Eden Apple Pie, sprinkle your own wishes and desires into the mixing bowl. As in the movie *Like Water for Chocolate*, these passion-inflamed spells will act as powerful adhesive, binding butter, sugar, and flour into practical, work-a-day aphrodisiacs. His senses will ignite, and with them a profound interest in the woman who is tending the fire.

By entrusting yourself to a cookbook stocked with the spirited ingredients of life, you can master the steps of a hypnotizing dance. First, pour him a glass of Irish Cream Moonshine to unbridle his passions (with such an elixir in your possession, the possibilities of romance are limitless). Next, knowing that soup warms the heart and nurtures the soul, tango his taste buds with a potent, amatory Aphrodite's Clam Chowder. As the dance continues, rhumba up the sustaining power of a luscious Love Apple Linguini, mated with Cleopatra's Caesar Salad and an aromatic slice of oven-kissed, homemade bread. Then, waltz casually ahead holding a silky slice of Casablanca Cheesecake that rivals any on earth. Last, present a whimsical and unusual lure such as homemade dog biscuits for his prized pooch or a tin of Pistachio Brittle (only if he likes pistachios!) for a late-night sweet tooth when he is back home dreaming of you.

By collecting inventive ideas, an inspired kitchen goddess can add spark to her recipes, and ultimately, to her romances. Skill, and a spicy sense of awareness, will enable you to pepper your cookbook collection with insightful modifications, anecdotes, and a journal account of personal discovery. Making a dedicated effort to *perfect* these ambrosial feats to your fancy should naturally spur you toward fashioning dazzling enhancements in your life. A true revelation might then occur: The search for fleeting affection has blossomed into an illuminated life of harmony and happiness—and candlelit tête-à-têtes—with a man who adores you. Your actions have been glorified by your gifts.

Then, it's time to beguile your passionate palates for the long haul. Consider this vision: You are charming an extraordinary paramour by gazing into his hungry eyes. Your very best, freshly baked chocolate chip cookies glow between you. As an added enticement, you have dabbed a hint of vanilla behind your ears (knowing Chanel No. 5 would have worked in a pinch). The atmosphere is aromatic and bewitching. Smiling, you nibble the edge of a scrumptious morsel and present the rest of the cookie to your eager male. After he has finished your coy offering and is *completely* mesmerized, invite him for a sweet, sweet kiss. The moment is mystical: You may not have expensive lipstick on your smile, but you will have a satisfied man in your arms.

Make your ongoing domestic life deliciously playful. Make Pasta with Ginger Shrimp Soul Sauce, and Risky Biscuits with Hot Tropics Pepper Chutney. Make the most enticing Never-Fail Uptown Chocolate Cake to ever brush the lips. Make breakfast-in-bed Finnish Dutch Babies. Make a wish. Make love.

The Art of Practical Seduction

After Aphrodite emerged triumphant in a tense beauty pageant against the jealous Hera and war-waging Athena and was awarded a golden apple inscribed "To the fairest" by a mortal man named Paris, that naughty and noble fruit—the apple—was forever infused with the power of her legendary passion. (For the spicy details on this story, turn to *The Golden Apple Invitational* on page 247.)

In giving the goddess of the Golden Apple her proper exultations, it is fitting to present a recipe infused with all the vital ingredients to keep deities and mortals alike singing its praises. It is sweet and laced with the goddess' insignia spice—cinnamon— and made with the Garden of Eden's most tempting harvest. You can serve these muffins in bed. They're *French*. My advice to you: Christen these sweet treats to reflect the name or nationality of your admirer or audience at hand.

French Apple-Spice Breakfast Muffins

Muffins

4½ cups unbleached white flour

1¾ cups sugar

1 tablespoon baking powder

¾ teaspoon salt

¾ teaspoon ground nutmeg

3 eggs

1½ cups milk

1 cup melted margarine

1 cup finely chopped or grated apple

Topping

1 cup sugar   1 tablespoon ground cinnamon

3 tablespoons melted butter

Preheat oven to 350°F. In a large bowl, mix all dry ingredients together and form a well in the center. Whisk the eggs and milk together and pour into the dry mixture. As you begin to combine mixtures gently, dribble the melted margarine around the sides of the bowl, working only until all ingredients come together. To avoid tough, cone-headed muffins, it is extremely important not to overmix. Gently fold in the apple.

Scoop dough into a muffin tin lined with muffin cups. Bake for 20 to 25 minutes or until a toothpick comes out clean. While the muffins are cooking, prepare the topping: Combine sugar and cinnamon and set aside; melt butter and set aside. Upon liberating the muffins from the oven, immediately brush the tops with melted butter and sprinkle with the cinnamon-sugar mixture as you cast your love spell.

Makes a baker's dozen (invest in a little heart-shaped tin in which to bake the thirteenth—and, I say, lucky—muffin).

He who is not impatient is not in love.

—Italian proverb

What can it be, that subtle treachery that lurks in tea cakes,
and is totally absent in the rude honesty of toast?

—John Ruskin

No Love Lost with This Sauce

For years, the traditional Saturday morning breakfast at the Mayfield House Bed and Breakfast in Tahoe City, California, was a delicious spin-off of a popular favorite—French toast. Weekend lovers would eagerly sprint from their rooms when the aroma of griddled, butter-kissed, spicy sweet bread wafted about the beams of the quaint dining room.

The secrets of my version of classic *pain perdu* ("lost bread" in French—a resourceful solution for those unloved loaves that have gone stale) are the bread, the spice, and the sauce. Unlike French baguettes, Portuguese bread—and its honeyed, tropical soul loaf, King's Hawaiian Bread—has a sweeter, more delicate texture, and is traditionally baked in large round loaves. Many recipes for French toast, such as the grandiose Texas toast, forego the spices altogether, and would never call for vanilla. It is the sauce, however—that hot, syrupy, sanctified sauce—that carries the magic and delivers the spell.

In the days of antiquity, sensuous, nectar-dripping apricots and peaches were believed to be the fruits of Venus, emitting energies of love, peace, health, and happiness. In China, a supernatural peach was responsible for turning a seventh-century goddess-heroine who ate of it into a fairy, thereby consigning her to a life of immortality and a diet of moonbeams and mother-of-pearl. Love Sauce is an aphrodisiac made by stewing ripe peaches or apricots in maple syrup or honey until the elixir is soft and mushy—and potent. After sampling this un-French toast, you may choose to remain in a Portuguese state of mind, drenched in Love Sauce for the rest of your breakfasting days.

Portuguese Toast with Love Sauce

4 large firm peaches or 8 apricots, peeled, pitted, and sliced

Approximately ¾ cup pure maple syrup

1 round loaf King's Hawaiian Bread or Portuguese sweet bread

1 teaspoon ground nutmeg, divided

4 eggs

1 cup half-and-half or milk

½ teaspoon ground cinnamon

½ teaspoon pure vanilla extract

Butter for frying

Powdered sugar (optional)

Place the fruit in a medium-sized saucepan, add maple syrup and sprinkle ½ teaspoon of the nutmeg over everything. Cover, and bring to a boil over medium-low heat. Once the syrup begins to boil, turn off the heat, but leave the saucepan on the burner to keep the nectar warm.

Slice the loaf of bread in half, then cut those halves in half, and cut those now-quarters into three pieces each, slicing off the very ends. (Got that? A loaf of King's provides 12 hefty 1-inch thick slices of bread of varied sizes, plus 4 ends definitely worth battering up and frying.) In a shallow bowl, whisk the eggs, half-and-half, remaining ½ teaspoon nutmeg, cinnamon, and vanilla together.

Melt a dollop of butter in a skillet or on a griddle over medium-high heat. Dip both sides of the bread quickly in the egg mixture and fry each slice for 2 to 3 minutes, until golden brown; flip and fry the other side. Serve toast on warmed plates, accompanied by a bowl of the Love Sauce. Sprinkle with a touch of powdered sugar for aesthetics, if you wish.

Serves 4.

A la Goddess

* File this easy formula for French toast in your mind: 1 large egg per person and ¼ cup milk or half-and-half per egg; add spices to taste. (If you are serving someone who can eat half a loaf of bread, you will have to scale everything up, of course.) Also, if you get caught in winter with no fresh peaches or apricots, don't hesitate to substitute thawed frozen fruit or fruit canned in unsweetened syrup (drained); you will need about 2 cups sliced peaches or apricots.

Full Moon Swamp Secrets

*T*he Frog. The Kiss. The Prince. Do you *believe* this outlandish tale we've been spoon-fed since we were old enough to say "Cinderella?" Okay, let's take off our glass slippers, let our hair down, and share our secrets. How many of you have actually *done the deed?* Be honest. Who has in *fact* planted a puckered wish on the lubricious lips of an amphibious paramour in a moment of passionate morbid curiosity?

Let me share the juicy secret: The best time to find frogs is during the full moon, and superstition again tells us that the frog-prince type of toad comes out only on blue moons. We all know that a blue moon is a full moon that shows its luminous soul for a second time in one month. And blinis are those cute little Russian pancakes with the funny-sounding name. Which has nothing to do with anything—fairy-tale logic, once again—unless of course, you want it to.

If the truth be liberated from my lips and pen, I'll admit that with a few well-spelled kisses—coupled with timely offerings of Love Apple Linguini, Cowboy Cookies, and Casablanca Cheesecake—I have transformed frogs into princes . . . or to something of that fabled nature.

Lily Pads with Blue Moon Blini Sauce

Lily Pads

1 cup buttermilk

1 egg

1 tablespoon butter, melted

2 tablespoons applesauce

1 cup unbleached white flour

½ teaspoon baking soda

½ teaspoon baking powder

Blue Moon Blini Sauce

1½ cups fresh blueberries
(frozen will do in a pinch)

⅓ cup brown sugar

3 to 4 tablespoons lemon juice,
freshly squeezed

Dash of ground nutmeg

First, make the batter for the Lily Pads. Whisk the buttermilk and egg together in a large bowl. Add the melted butter, applesauce, and salt and mix well. Measure out the flour, blend the soda and baking powder into it, and add to the buttermilk mixture. Blend well, then let the batter rest for 5 minutes.

Make the sauce. In a saucepan on medium-high heat, mix blueberries, sugar, lemon juice, and nutmeg together. Bring to a boil, reduce heat, and simmer, stirring, for about 5 minutes or until the sauce begins to thicken.

When you are ready to make the pancakes, lightly grease a griddle or pan and heat over medium heat. Ladle small, 3-inch pools of batter into the griddle or pan. Cook until teeny bubbles come to the surface, then flip. Serve Lily Pads on a large, colorful plate and top them with the Blue Moon Sauce.

Makes 16 pancakes, but the batter and sauce will keep refrigerated for days, so cook up as many or as few as you desire.

A la Goddess

* Each Lily Pad bestows one wish. With your newly transformed prince, take turns making wishes or celebrating wishes that have been manifested. If you haven't kissed the proper toad yet and are enjoying your Lily Pads alone, make a wish for yourself with each embracing, safely-in-the-brightest-moments-of-childhood, satisfying bite.

Like a Baby's . . .

*F*rolicsome, yet sensuous, the following recipe begs to be eaten when in the nude, or at least when wrapped in silk scarves or sporting a silky garb of some sort. The recipe simply possesses a texture that complements such buffed fashion. If this dish manifested itself in human form, Finnish Dutch Babies would be naked little cherubs floating about the dining table.

Originally called a "Finnish pancake," this cream puff of a pancake was the Sunday specialty at the same bed and breakfast inn that served Portuguese Toast. Some visitors were known to stay an extra night solely to experience the ritual of this meal. Usually it was shared between lovers, and those of us serving it were often amused by the squabbles over the last bite. These were the candid-camera moments that would reap the grand prize on *America's Funniest Home Videos*. Of course, you could always request your very own Finnish Dutch Baby and eliminate the obligation to share.

It is rare to unearth a good recipe for authentic Finnish Dutch Babies (it's one of the few recipes that the *Joy of Cooking* doesn't have), so this is a dandy worth mastering. And, for those of us who wonder why they are called "Dutch Babies" or "Finnish pancakes," I implore anyone who *does* know to write me and tell me. I have heard so many myths that I start to get dizzy trying to sort them out. I will say this about these babies, as Dr. Spock once said about the other kind of babies, "You know more than you think you do."

Finnish Dutch Babies

4 tablespoons honey	1 cup unbleached white flour
4 eggs	2 cups milk
½ teaspoon salt	4 tablespoons butter, melted
1 cup half-and-half	

Preheat oven to 350°F. Whisk all ingredients, except the melted butter, together in a bowl. Pour the melted butter into an 8-inch glass pie plate and swirl it around, coating the sides of the plate. Delicately pour or ladle the batter into the pie plate. Cook for 20 minutes or until this "baby" looks like a giant popover. Open and close the oven door slowly and with great care or the popover will "poof" into a heart-breaking, deflated mess.

A LA GODDESS

* This creature is intended to be served in the pie plate and shared by two people
who like each other. Dress the baby up with a small side bowl of sliced strawberries

or apple slices sautéed in a bit of butter, a few shakes of ground ginger, and a pinch of nutmeg. I can't imagine it, but if someone doesn't care to share from the same plate, split the batter into two smaller glass pie plates and prevent fork fights.

C'est du pipi d'ange

In her linguistic banquet of a book, *Ladyfingers and Nun's Tummies: A Lighthearted Look at How Foods Got Their Names,* Martha Barnette serves a smörgasbörd of chatty food lore and playful etymology. After indulging in this celebration of words and food, you'll find a reason to giggle when eating tortellini, savoring umbilichi sacri, "the goddess' belly button," or baking with walnuts, scientifically known as Jovis glans, or "Jove's acorn"— yep, you guessed it.

Prepare to satiate your senses with this self-described "deipnosophist's delight." You'll learn that dates are really finger-apples, that the Brits see ladyfingers as boudoir biscuits, and that the German translation for butterfly is "milk thief" while the Dutch describe this milk-filching fairy as *boterschijte* or "butter s—" . . . okay, we won't go there. Rather, take a celestial tour through the world of *angel's food* (a light, white cake), *angel's pie* (lingonberry and whipped cream pie), *angels on horseback* (bacon-wrapped oysters on toast), *angel hair* (pasta), *angel's breasts* ("a heavenly dessert"), an *angel's kiss* (a cocktail), and—forgive me—*angel's piss,* a fine French wine.

The Romaine Empire, Lightly Tossed

Cleopatra, queen of Egypt and goddess-by-proxy, seemed to know how to enjoy herself—especially when conquering men's hearts, their integrity, lands, and empires. I envision her basking by the pool, with gorgeous, bare-chested male slaves fanning her with palm fronds, rubies resting on her eyes in place of RayBans, and her cell phone ringing, heralding news of the latest land deal.

We are all aware that she shared her last meal with Marc Antony and an asp, but we must wonder what she did to first seduce the great Julius Caesar. Did she simply purr, "If you give me your armies and their general, I'll make you a dynamite dinner?" Whatever she promised, or had whipped up in her palatial kitchen—if we looked between the hieroglyphics we might discover the true origin of the Caesar Salad—her lusty legacy lives on.

Cleopatra's Caesar Salad

1 head Romaine lettuce, washed and patted dry

2 to 4 anchovy fillets

Juice of half a lemon

¼ cup extra virgin olive oil

¼ teaspoon sea salt

Croutons (optional)

⅓ to ½ cup freshly grated Parmesan or Romano cheese

3 cloves garlic, finely minced

1 egg, raw or coddled (directions follow)

¼ teaspoon freshly ground black pepper

Few shakes dry mustard

Mash the anchovies and garlic together with a fork in a small bowl to make a paste. Transfer to a large wooden salad bowl, and whisk in the lemon juice and egg. Add the olive oil and whisk until blended. Blend in salt, pepper, mustard, and about half of the cheese. Add the lettuce and toss until each leaf is well coated. Arrange on a chilled platter and sprinkle with remaining cheese. Garnish with garlic croutons and another anchovy fillet if you feel the urge.

Serves 2.

A la Goddess

* To coddle an egg, bring 1 to 2 inches of water to a lively boil in a small saucepan. Turn off heat. Using a slotted spoon, lower the egg into the water and let it stand for 1 minute. Remove and let cool before breaking into the salad.

* Reed Scranton, a kitchen goddess in Boston, suggests adding a dash of cayenne pepper and oregano. "The secret to a great Caesar Salad," she says, "is having a special wooden bowl used only for the Caesar. Your bowl will be seasoned more and more every time you make the dressing."

* For those of you who are afflicted with an aversion to anchovies, substitute 1 to 2 tablespoons Worcestershire sauce (to taste) for these salty sea monsters. But beware of losing the aphrodisiacal quality.

Beet-Red Beauty Secrets

*I*n the joyously outlandish novelette *Jitterbug Perfume* by Tom Robbins, we discover the salubrious secrets of immortality: deep and proper breathing, frequent bouts of tantric sex, and beets. Beets—a vegetable of such indescribable scarlet-vermilion hue that one can truly only describe it by name: beet red. Not surprisingly, considering their colorful lure and potent powers, beets were the goddess Aphrodite's beauty secret; how she used them to increase and prolong her beauty we can only imagine.

The Russians, heeding this knowledge, are renowned for cooking up bottomless pots of immortality, beauty, and virility called *borscht*. Also extolling the potency of borscht is Carla Wheeler and best pal Cassidy. When Carla shared this old family recipe with me, she said with a deep breath, "I love it. Best soup ever! Beautiful color!" If you got a glimpse of Carla—vibrant, lustrous, ruby-blond—you might be convinced that this praiseworthy beauty secret is real.

There is no spectacle on earth more appealing than that of
a beautiful woman in the act of cooking dinner for someone she loves.
Thus the sight . . . was enough to drive him mad with love and hunger.

—Thomas Wolfe, *April, Late April*

C's Ruby Soup

6 cans (14½ ounces each) chicken broth
(or 11 cups stock)

1 dozen beets, diced, with beet leaves,
chopped (discard stems)

2 to 3 heads red cabbage, chopped

4 to 6 onions, chopped

12 carrots, peeled and diced

½ cup vinegar

½ pound (1 bunch) spinach leaves,
chopped

3 bay leaves

1 tablespoon dried parsley leaves

2 teaspoons salt

1 teaspoon black pepper

Sour cream

6 shakes lemon pepper

Place all ingredients except sour cream in a large pot and simmer for at least 3 hours (all day is even better). Serve with sour cream.

Makes 8 to 10 servings.

The Foods of Love

Clams, oysters, mushrooms, bananas, artichokes, seafood, tomatoes, apples, parsley, chili powder, nutmeg, cinnamon, asparagus, truffles, chocolate, Champagne, *the imagination* . . . the list of aphrodisiacs, those edible sex-inducing delicacies named for the goddess herself, is as long as the brain waves of the person making it.

Yes, we've all been told it's the potassium and the zinc—so essential to sustaining virility; or it's the priapic proportions, the convenient shape, and the stimulating color—sexually suggestive, erotic, visually exciting. I now understand it's also the texture and the temperature—creamy, viscous, oozing, dripping, warm. It's the expectation and anticipation. It's the exotic blends of ingredients and aroma. With Aphrodite's Clam Chowder and Banana Salsa Swordfish, it's the taste.

Aphrodite's Clam Chowder

1¼ pounds (3 to 4 medium) potatoes, diced and cooked

3 cans (6½-ounces each) chopped clams, drained; juice reserved

2 tablespoons clam base (found in specialty stores, see below for substitute)

½ cup unbleached white flour

¼ cup butter, melted

7 cups half-and-half or milk

2 teaspoons minced garlic

2 teaspoons sugar

Salt and pepper to taste

Using a large bain-marie or double-boiler, heat the half-and-half (or milk), garlic, clam base*, clam juice (strained from the can), and sugar to a hot simmer.

(In a double boiler, this mixture will not come to a boil.)

In a small bowl, combine the butter and flour to form a roux. Whisk the roux gently into the simmering clam concoction. Cook for 10 to 15 minutes until the mixture begins to thicken. Add the clams and cooked potatoes and simmer for another 5 to 10 minutes.

Serves 4.

A la Goddess

* To make a substitute for the clam base, purée the contents of a 6½-ounce can of clams with 1 tablespoon salt and 2 teaspoons lemon juice; use 2 tablespoons of this mixture.

Banana Salsa Swordfish

1 bunch cilantro (about 4-ounces), stems removed, finely chopped; about 1 cup

1-inch piece ginger root, peeled and grated

2 to 3 firm bananas, diced

1 red bell pepper, chopped

1 jalapeño pepper, chopped

1 tablespoon brown sugar

Juice of 1½ limes

Salt and pepper

2 fresh swordfish or mahimahi steaks, each about 1-inch thick

1 tablespoon flour

2 teaspoons freshly ground pepper

Olive oil

2 tablespoons butter

¼ cup white wine or sherry

Salt and pepper

To make the salsa, combine cilantro, ginger, bananas, red pepper, jalapeño, brown sugar, lime juice, and salt and pepper to taste. Set aside to marinate while you prepare the fish.

Dredge the steaks in flour and grind pepper onto the surface. Press the pepper into the fish with the heel of your hand, then lightly brush with olive oil. Melt butter in a sauté or frying pan. Stir in the wine. Fry fish over medium heat until golden brown on one side; flip over and brown the other side. Salt and pepper to taste. (The complete cooking time will be approximately 10 minutes per inch thickness of fish.) Serve steaks bountifully garnished with banana salsa.

Serves 2.

A la Goddess

* Mahimahi, a lighter, flakier fish, is also superb with this eclectic salsa. A Caesar salad for the appetizer and a well-made Margarita chaser or a glass of cold, nutty Chardonnay transport this entrée to the top of my list of Kitchen Goddess' all-time favorite romantic dinners.

* You can also grill the fish; it will eliminate the sauté process and add yet another dimension to the flavor and flair of this dish. Also, feel free to sauté the fish in wine with less (or no) butter.

* Whenever I increase this recipe to accommodate more people, I add a green bell pepper to the banana salsa to heighten the hue.

The Goddess Takes a Holiday

O
n an average day in the heavens, surely the ungodly soap-opera antics on Mount Olympus could catch up with any worship-weary goddess: the king of the heavens Zeusing about—debauching, whipping lightning bolts around, ravishing unsuspecting downtown goddesses and lovely mortals, and playing hide and seek with his consort, Hera; their sanguinary and aggressive son Ares, the god of war, pushing everyone's immortal buttons; Hades harassing Persephone and her mother; a drunk Dionysus chasing wood nymphs. The wise princess of paradise would simply pack up and plan a quick get-away. But if she is already living high on the hill, intoxicated with ambrosia and nectar, where does a goddess go to vacation?

Slovenia. Honest. There is a folktale in this little-known land that tells of Slovenia's creation: After the goddess created heaven, she had a small amount of magical dust remaining. As she fondly regarded her next creation, earth, she sprinkled this angel-dust, and made the most beautiful of all places—Slovenia. It has been said that life is composed of happy accidents and divine revelations. Slovenia, a place of mythical treasures, incomparable natural beauty, and medieval castles on distant hillsides framed by awe-inspiring alpine peaks, is a rare revelation.

I had never *dreamed* of Slovenia until I fell under the spell of a young, debonair Slovenian ski-racing demigod when he prepared for me a captivating native novelty of fruit-filled boiled dumplings. This taste of Slovenia was curiously intriguing, as was the chef; I decided to stay for a second, and a third, and a fourth . . . helping. He's now my husband. If any of the goddesses of old had been fortunate enough to meet him and sample his darling of a dish, I'm sure the recipe for plum dumplings—and the cook—would have been whisked back to the Mount Olympus Café.

Slovenian Plum Dumplings

2 medium potatoes

2½ cups cottage cheese, drained of excess liquid

2 eggs

¾ teaspoon salt

2 cups unbleached white flour

8 small, ripe, fresh purple plums or apricots, pitted

½ cup bread crumbs

3 to 4 tablespoons oil or melted butter

Brown sugar

Ground cinnamon and nutmeg to taste

Peel the potatoes, quarter them, and boil until tender. Mash until smooth and let cool a bit. Add to the cottage cheese and mix well. Beat in the eggs and salt. Work enough flour into the mixture to form a smooth, firm dough.

Bring a large pot of water to a rolling boil over high medium heat. Spoon about ½ cup of dough into your hand. (To prevent the dough from sticking, run your hands under cold water before forming each dumpling.) Pat the dough into a round cake and place a piece of fruit in the center. Then pat and fold the dough over and around it (as if you were making a snowball), completely sealing the fruit within the dough ball.

Drop the dumplings, one at a time, in the pot of boiling water. After the water returns to a boil once all the dumplings are in it, cook gently for at least 12 minutes (the dumplings will float to the surface as they cook). Gently scoop them out with a slotted spoon and place in a large serving bowl.

In a small skillet, mix the bread crumbs with the oil or butter, and sauté over medium heat until crisp. Garnish the dumplings with this mixture, sprinkle them with brown sugar, nutmeg, and cinnamon, and serve hot.

Makes 8 dumplings.

A la Goddess

* If fresh fruit is not in season, fruit canned in natural, unsweetened syrup works well. Drain off the syrup. My chef usually uses apricot halves when he uses canned fruit.

* My preference changes from batch to batch, but I often favor these dumplings without potatoes, especially if I'm uninterested in putting forth the extra potato-prep effort or I'm eating less starch that day. Simply omit the earth apples and add a bit more flour; expect your yield to be one less dumpling. It truly is a matter of heritage and taste genetics, I think. My chef's mom makes them without the cottage cheese (increase potatoes to 5 medium or 2½ cups mashed). I wonder which dumplings he really favors?

Leave a kiss but in the cup,
And I'll not look for wine.

—Ben Jonson, *To Celia*

I used to take cooking classes when I was younger . . .
because girls weren't interested in me and
I thought I may be alone for the rest of my life.

—Michael Jordan

Sexy Fried Green Tomatoes

*P*ommes d'amour, *Liebesäpfel*, love apples. Legend holds that these brilliantly colored vegetables that so resemble the other esteemed passion fruit—apples—do indeed harbor ultrapowerful aphrodisiacal enzymes. The nickname "love apple" is of course derived from the French *pommes d'amour;* the French, always quick to color life with amorous inferences, misunderstood the Italian word for tomato, *pomodoro,* or "fruit of gold" and named the tomato with a phonetic twin phrase. Whichever way you fry 'em—fried green tomatoes or fried gold love apples—hell, they really don't even have to be green or gold—this desirable dish has kept many a man coming back for more of *something.*

I won't deny that other versions of this popular Dixieland classic have made it big on other plates, in hot spots of other cookbooks, and even in their own movie, but this rendition unquestionably carries a tune of its own. And again, whether it's the singer or the song, just about everyone I know loves this tune.

Love Apple Linguini

1 package (1 pound) linguini

1 cup unbleached white flour

¼ cup cornmeal

2 teaspoons dried basil

1 teaspoon dill

1 teaspoon curry powder

½ teaspoon pepper

Salt to taste

1 tablespoon butter

1 tablespoon olive oil

2 cloves garlic, pressed or minced

1¼ cups milk

¼ cup wine (white *or* red, depending on
your whim and what is in the house)

3 big, fat, very firm tomatoes of any color, cut
into ¼-inch slices

Prepare the pasta, according to package directions, in a large pot of boiling water. While the pasta is cooking, fry the tomatoes.

In a plastic container with a lid combine flour, cornmeal, basil, dill, curry powder, pepper, and salt, cover with the lid, and shake, mixing all ingredients well. Melt butter and oil together in a large skillet over medium-high heat. As the skillet heats up, add garlic. Place tomato slices in the container, 2 at a time, and shake back and forth and up and down until they are completely coated with flour mixture. Plop them in the frying pan.

Fry for 4 to 5 minutes, then gently flip *les pommes d'amour* and fry for a few minutes more (if the pan seems dry pour in a little milk or wine as you are turning the tomatoes over). Remove them from skillet and set on a large serving plate. See to it that the tomatoes are kept warm (I either microwave them or keep them in a heated oven, uncovered)—we want them crisp!

Reduce heat to medium low and pour the rest of the milk and wine into the still-hot skillet, whisking as you pour. After heating the sauce a bit, slowly sprinkle about ¼ cup of the remaining flour mixture into the pan, stirring constantly to avoid lumps. As the sauce begins to bubble and thicken, add more flour mixture if necessary to make a nice, creamy, flowing gravy. When it reaches this point, remove sauce from heat and pour into a fine china gravy boat or decorative serving bowl.

Drain the pasta, toss it with a little olive oil, and divide among 4 dinner plates. Spoon several *pommes d'amour* on top of the pasta, and smother them with the sauce. Salt and pepper to suit your taste.

Serves 4.

The only victory over love is flight.

—Napoleon

Two things are essential in life:
to give good dinners and
to keep on fair terms with women.

—Tallyrand

Cult of Salt

From Roman Catholic priests dabbing it on the unsuspecting tongues of innocent babes at baptisms to New Age seers using it during invocations and purification rites to the superstitious tossing it over the left shoulder to ward off evil, salt basks on its own altar in the minds of mortals. This edible rock carries with it a history and power like no other substance in the kitchen. The cult of salt has faithful adherents from every corner of the world, each culture infusing its own customs, beliefs, and applications to this crystallized stone. In fact, it was even used as currency in Roman times (the Eternal City was founded on the salt trade), and any traitor caught selling it to the enemy was punished with death.

In her book *Much Depends on Dinner*, author Margaret Visser honors salt with an entire chapter dedicated to the history, lore, technical information, and symbolic bravado of our favorite flavoring agent. She highlights the delightfully salty folktale that eventually inspired Shakespeare's *King Lear*. After a young princess tells her father, the king, that she loves him not like gold and silver but "like salt," he banishes her from the kingdom in a fury of "in-salted" rage. When she marries, she invites the king (who does not know the identity of the bride behind the veil) to the wedding and orders all food be prepared without salt. Finding the food reproachfully bland, he weeps at his harsh judgment of his daughter. Upon revealing herself by adding a pinch of salt to his meal, she enlivens both his life and his palate; they reconcile and live happily ever after.

Salt preserves from corruption, symbolically seals friendships and covenants, sharpens the mind and the intellect, and "counteracts the malediction" of sorcerers and bad spirits—evil witches and devils hate it. One of salt's more pleasurable properties, attributed to Aphrodite, the "sea-foam born" goddess who sprang from the ocean—salt's quintessential home "surf"—is its reputed ability to cure a man's impotence if a band of wild women rubs his uncooperative member with this great rock of ages.

Thou hast no faults,
or I no faults can spy;
Thou art all beauty,
or all blindness I.

—Anonymous

Romancing the Robe

*F*ewer tales satiate our ravenous imaginations as well as that of an impassioned, clandestine love affair between a priest and an ex-nun. Deem it a legendary Shakespearean-spiced love steeped in risk, honor, and fate, or dismiss it as tabloid fodder, a taboo-busting story like this leaves a breezy sense of bravado in its wake. If these two paramours had met on a bridge in Madison County, she would have left the stew pot boiling over on the stove, he would have tossed his camera in the cornfield, and together they would have jumped from that bridge and skinny-dipped down the river of life.

He was a handsome, dynamic, young Catholic priest saving souls on Chicago's turbulent Southside. She had just traded her habit for a miniskirt and was leaving her convent after almost a decade. Surrounded by the terrazzo tiles and beige walls of a humid church basement, he fatefully asked to borrow her fineline Bic pen; she noticed how tan he looked in his lemon yellow shirt; he simply *noticed*.

The *coup de foudre* only intensified when they discovered they were stationed in neighboring parishes. She would sit out on a larger-than-life tree stump waiting to be picked up by her knight in his red, shining, Plymouth Barracuda chariot. They would zip off to Café Diana, a favorite goddess-graced Greek restaurant, and talk for hours over feta cheese and olive salads and bottles of red Rhoditis wine. Evenings would end on one of many enchanted Lake Michigan beachfronts, the sand their dance floor, the waves the music, and the moon their muse, under which they wrote poetry. Good-bye Plato, hello Zorba!

He proposed with an aluminum soda can ring, they married, had six kids, were reincarnated as toy inventors, and sauntered off into their sunset. Though the dance may not be as agile after thirty years and counting, Father Charm and Sister Charmed are still soul mates who love to be with each other—on the sand, near the sea, or at their kitchen table lingering over their favorite pasta dish.

The following impetuous meal of Pasta with Ginger Shrimp Soul Sauce accompanied by Risky Biscuits, dressed with Hot Tropics Pepper Chutney and crowned with a luscious dessert of Irish Cream Moonshine presents an irreverent combination of contrasting flavors that prove themselves splendidly by moonlight or candlelight. With a morsel of inventive creativity—or *inventivity*, a term consecrated by our two lovers—this tasty mélange can be completed in less time than it takes to fall in love. Prepare the Chutney and Moonshine days in advance, bake a big batch of biscuits before the sun sets, and warm them up in the oven or microwave while blending the sauce, which takes eleven minutes or less. The secret is to share it with someone you adore.

Pasta with Ginger Shrimp Soul Sauce

½ pound pasta; small shells or farfalle (butterflies) are nice

1 tablespoon butter

1 tablespoon finely chopped sweet onions

½ pound bay shrimp

1 medium tomato, coarsely chopped

1 mango, diced

¼ teaspoon (about 8 shakes) paprika

1 teaspoon ground ginger

1¼ cups milk, at room temperature

1 tablespoon unbleached white flour

Parmigiano-Reggiano cheese, freshly grated

Sea salt

Prepare pasta according to package directions. In a large skillet, melt the butter and sauté the shrimp for 1 minute over medium heat. Add onion and sauté for a few more minutes. Add the mango and tomato, sprinkle with ginger and paprika and continue to sauté for 2 to 3 minutes more. Add the milk and cook until bubbling. Sprinkle flour evenly over the mixture, stirring briskly to prevent lumps. Season with salt and cook until the sauce thickens. Serve over pasta with freshly grated Parmigiano-Reggiano, and accompanied by a glass of fine wine. Serves 2.

Risky Biscuits

2 cups unbleached white flour

¾ teaspoon salt

¼ teaspoon baking soda

1 tablespoon baking powder

2 teaspoons sugar (optional)

⅓ cup solid vegetable shortening (butter flavored Crisco is great!), chilled

Melted butter (optional)

¾ cup buttermilk

Heat oven to 450°F. In a large bowl, combine the flour, salt, baking soda, baking powder, and optional sugar. Cut the cold shortening into the flour mixture with a pastry blender or a large, wide-tined fork until coarse crumbs form. Add the buttermilk, tossing with a fork until a dough forms.

Turn the dough out onto a lightly floured surface, form it into a disk, and knead a few times. (Red light! Red light! If you want those flaky, melt-in-your-mouth, good ol' southern hallmark biscuits, don't overhandle the dough. All sorts of petty variables have the power to toughen up the biscuits: too much flour on the rolling board, too much kneading; an oven that's too tepid—things like that. Be attentive to your craft and you will avoid rock biscuits.) Without using a lot of muscle, roll the dough—from the center out—to ¾-inch thickness. Cut out biscuits of a desired size with a cookie or biscuit cutter. Gather the dough trimmings, pat to the proper thickness, and cut out more biscuits.

Place biscuits about 2 inches apart (closer if you like soft-sided biscuits) on an ungreased baking sheet. Bake until a golden brown, about 12 to 15 minutes. Brush with melted butter for the full, authentic, down-home effect.

Makes 12 to 18 biscuits.

Hot Tropics Pepper Chutney

2 firm but ripe mangos, peeled and chopped

¼ cup raisins

2 cups fresh pineapple, finely chopped or crushed

⅔ cup brown sugar

⅔ cup apple cider or red currant vinegar

Half a red onion, finely chopped

1 jalapeño pepper, seeds and ribs removed, chopped

Juice of 1 lemon

½-inch piece ginger root, peeled and grated

1 teaspoon ground cinnamon

1 firm papaya, peeled, seeded and diced

½ teaspoon red pepper flakes

½ teaspoon ground ginger

½ teaspoon ground cloves

Combine all ingredients, except ginger and cloves, and bring to a boil in a large heavy saucepan over medium-low heat. Stir often to prevent burning. Reduce heat to low, add ground ginger and cloves, cover, and simmer for 1 to 1½ hours, stirring every 15 or 20 minutes to add a little energy and prevent burning.

Cool completely before serving. Serve in a decorative side dish with a chutney spoon if you have one. (If you don't, put one on your Christmas list—they are quaint little utensils.) Store in sterilized jars or refrigerate. (This chutney is also superb with crab cakes or anything with a little crunch to it, such as crackers, crisp bread, or fritters.)

Makes approximately 1 quart.

Irish Cream Moonshine

This legendary nectar of forest fairies, leprechauns, and tree sprites is guaranteed to make the moonbeams brighter, the starshine lighter, and the love life mightier. When you begin dallying with the sprites instead of your date, you've probably had enough.

I can (14 ounces) sweetened, condensed milk

1 cup half-and-half

3 tablespoons chocolate syrup

2 eggs

2 teaspoons instant coffee crystal

2 teaspoons pure vanilla extract

½ teaspoon almond extract

1¾ cups Irish whiskey

¼ cup dark rum

Blend all ingredients, except the booze, together in a blender or with a whisk. Add whiskey and rum and mix vigorously. Pour into bottle or decanter and store refrigerated.

Makes approximately 12 half-cup fairy-sized servings.

May the day keep fine for you;
May the path to hell grow green for lack of travelers;
May you die at the age of ninety-five years
in bed with your lover, shot by a jealous spouse.

—Irish blessing

Don't Deliver Us from Temptation

*C*her chocolata, the grand-goddess of amatory love potions, presides in many a courtship ritual, and rarely fails to leave a trail of bliss behind her. She has been known to make exclusive, up-and-downtown appearances in American mating customs like nowhere else on this passion-pandering planet: Consider the Hershey's Kiss, the chocolate malt, the chocolate fudge brownie, the classic chocolate chip cookie, the chocolate Easter bunny, chocolate decadence, *devil's food* chocolate . . .

Before I even learned to practice kissing on the back of my hand, one of my favorite dessert combinations for flavor, color, and intrigue was classic devil's food cake with mocha frosting. When I discovered that this favorite, rich, sumptuous, semisweet, dark chocolate cupcake of kiddom was called *devil's food*, I was ready to turn in my rosary and march straight to the nearest bakery in Hades—they could keep their *angel food*.

This kissing cousin of the deepest, darkest devil's food cake imaginable can practically be made blindfolded by anyone, anywhere, in any stage of delirium. Whip it up for a *ménage à deux* sometime soon.

Never-Fail Uptown Chocolate Cake

4½ cups unbleached white flour

2¼ cups white sugar

½ cup unsweetened cocoa

1½ teaspoons salt

1 tablespoon baking soda

3 cups boiling water

3 eggs, beaten

1½ cups oil

1½ teaspoons pure vanilla extract

Mucho Mocha Frosting

½ cup heavy whipping cream

3 tablespoons instant coffee

2 tablespoons unsweetened cocoa

2 teaspoons pure vanilla extract

1½ cups butter, softened

4½ cups powdered sugar

Preheat oven to 350°F. Combine the flour, sugar, cocoa, and salt in a large mixing bowl and blend well. Separately, dissolve the baking soda in the boiling water and set aside. Place the eggs, oil, and vanilla in the center of the dry ingredients and mix together briefly. While mixing at medium speed using even and rhythmic motions, slowly pour the baking soda and water into the bowl. Mix until batter looks smooth, *but don't mix until it becomes bubbly*. Pour the batter into a well-oiled and floured 15-by-10-by-2¼-inch cake pan, filling pan two-thirds full.

Bake for 30 to 35 minutes. The cake is done when a toothpick inserted in the center comes out clean, and/or a finger gently pressed on the top leaves no indentation. Cool before frosting.

To make the frosting, mix the cream, coffee, cocoa, and vanilla together and set aside. Cream the butter and the sugar. Gradually beat in the coffee-cream mixture until smooth.

Yields enough frosting to accommodate the Never-Fail Uptown Chocolate Cake in all its incarnations.

A LA GODDESS

*The recipe can be accommodated in the following pans: three 8-inch round or heart-shaped pans (baking time: 20 to 25 minutes); 4 triple-layer baby cakes (clean tuna fish cans work well) or 2 dozen cupcakes (baking time: 15 minutes).

* To construct rich chocolate, picture-perfect layered baby cakes, remove the cakes from their pans after they have cooled, wrap them, and freeze them. After they are frozen, take a very sharp knife and trim down the mounds so you have flat surfaces. Stack the cakes three-high, adhering with frosting. Finally, frost the sides of the cake and decorate with candies, shaved chocolate, coconut, or chopped nuts. The temptation is delivered unto your lips—Indulge!

Though she is a lifelong vegetarian who never smoked nor drank,
[artist Beatrice] Wood, [age 104]
assigns less abstemious reasons for her longevity:
"Chocolate and young men."

—Hunter Drohojowska Philp, *Arts and Antiques*

God made men transparent; that way,
you are able to look right through a man
and see a god standing behind him.

—Needa Stanton

The Icing on the Cake

Grandma would have called it *icing*, but this is one of the greatest all-purpose, won't-ever-let-you-down *frosting* recipes I know. Slather it on everything from the Never-Fail Uptown Chocolate Cake to shortbread or the elegant Italian Cream Cake. Or frost your fingers and forgo the cake.

Butter-Cream Frosting

½ pound butter, softened

6 cups powdered sugar

1½ teaspoons pure vanilla extract

½ teaspoon lemon juice, optional

½ cup plus 2 tablespoons half-and-half or milk

With an electric mixer on low speed, cream the butter, sugar, vanilla, and lemon juice. Slowly add the half-and-half or milk until the frosting is creamy. Beat well but do not overmix or the frosting will separate and clump. Ice up the object of your desire and enjoy! Will frost one 9-inch 2-layer cake.

Wheresoever she was,
there was Eden.

    —Mark Twain

Just One Bite, Baby

*I*f the truth in history were known, we would discover that it was not an apple with which Eve tempted Adam that fateful day in Paradise, but rather a hot, bubbling, succulent, homemade apple pie. He simply had no choice. I know the power of this recipe, and I advise all to use it wisely and carefully, and always with the best of intentions. After all, women have been enticing men, and men have been seducing women, ever since that infamous picnic dessert—winner of the Paradise State Fair Purple Ribbon—was shared in Eden. I now entrust you with an updated version of that same temptation.

Garden of Eden Apple Pie

Dough

2 cups unbleached white flour

1¼ teaspoons salt

¼ teaspoon baking powder

½ cup *cold* Crisco shortening

⅓ cup *cold* margarine or butter (I prefer margarine)

⅓ cup *ice* water

7 or 8 McIntosh or Golden Delicious
  apples

⅔ cup raw sugar

2 tablespoons unbleached white flour

2 teaspoons ground cinnamon

I teaspoon ground nutmeg

2 teaspoons lemon juice

I teaspoon pure vanilla extract
  (optional)

Pinch of salt

Topping

¼ cup unbleached white flour

¼ cup raw sugar

3 tablespoons chilled butter

I teaspoon ground cinnamon

Make dough first. Blend dry ingredients together. Cut in the margarine or butter and shortening with a fork or pastry cutter until you achieve a fine, crumbly texture. Dribble the ice water over the flour mixture and mix together with a fork or by tossing with your hands quickly and lightly. Form 2 dough balls. Roll one ball to a ⅛-inch thickness and line a 10-inch deep-dish glass or ceramic pie plate.

Peel, core, and slice apples. (A Back to Basics brand apple peeler—available through L. L. Bean—makes this task quick and simple. Another option is to entice an onlooker to help you by offering the reward of the first slice of pie after it is done—works every time.)

Toss the apples, sugar, flour, spices, lemon juice, vanilla, and salt together. If you wish to cast any spells or add special intentions to your pie, do that now. Delicately line the pie shell with the apple mixture, gently pressing it into shape. Mix the topping ingredients together, using a fork to cut in the chilled butter, until the mixture takes on a crumbly texture. Sprinkle it on top of the apples.

Heat oven to 400°F. Roll out the second ball of dough and place it on top of your pie. Use a tiny quantity of cold water to stick the top crust to the bottom crust. Cut decorative slits on top for steam to escape. Cut off excess dough, leaving about 1 inch of dough to turn under and flute.

With the leftover pie dough, roll out and cut out hearts, the letters I and U, or any other special symbol you may have in mind. Seal your message of love to the top of the pie using a touch of water. Sprinkle a little raw sugar on top.

Bake at 400°F for 10 minutes. Reduce heat to 350°F and bake for 50 more minutes, or until pie is a desired golden brown color and apples are a perfect texture. Serve with a scoop of temptation.

Makes 1 double-crust pie; serves 8.

A la Goddess

* I *always* conserve my time and make enough dough for three double-crust or six single-crust pies. This dough freezes perfectly for up to a couple of weeks if wrapped securely in double plastic Ziploc bags. When multiplying the dough recipe by three, triple all the other ingredients, but use only ½ teaspoon baking powder and add an extra pinch of salt.

* Remember, pie dough is a cold dough. It stays flakiest and "melts-in-your-mouth" most delicately if handled as little as possible. (If you like to get your hands in dough and goosh it through your fingers, please take that pleasure in kneading the Olympic Squaw Bread, Hawaiian Sweet Potato Bread.) Always roll pastry dough on a well-floured, cool surface (marble is supreme). Roll gently with sweeping strokes from the center of the dough to the outer edge.

  To secure the top crust to the bottom crust, dab with cold water, which acts as Super Glue.

Knowing you is such delicious torment.

—Ralph Waldo Emerson

When Love Dishes Up a Plate of Fate

*D*eem it star-crossed, ill-fated, foredoomed, or simply shoddy timing, there are tales throughout eternity of the two lovers who, after a melt-down of reason and passion-infused love are forever destined to a life asunder. As the Fates—Clotho the Spinner, Lachesis the Dispenser of Lots, and Atropos the Inexorable—would have it, destiny was to be no darling to many a mortal couple: Juliet and her Romeo; Cleo and Marc Anthony; Joe DiMaggio and his Marilyn; Liz and Dick; Charles and Diana. Like fevered felines playing with their panting prey, those three goddesses could deal a wicked blow with their paws of providence . . . and fate would take its course.

In her bouncing, pleasure-driven, insouciant approach to life, Aphrodite was often a lightning rod for the Fates because of her mockery of the immortals and her rebellious defiance. We can almost envision her flipping her celestial mane and quipping, "Tomorrow is another day." When caught in flagrante delicto with her lover Ares and captured in a net by a jealous husband, she laughed. After all, as goddess of love and passion, she was just doing her job. When the goddess Persephone had the hots for Aphrodite's beloved Adonis, the love goddess agreed to shared him for half the year—but *she* got him in summer.

It is said Aphrodite loved mortal men and she took great pleasure in helping them woo mortal women. But to those who thought they were above the call of love, she was swift to serve an unpalatable plate of retribution. Her punishment for Eos, the goddess of dawn, was to cause Eos to fall in love with two mortal men at once, a great cause of amorous indigestion. Such was also the destiny of Ilsa in the town of Casablanca; her adoration of Rick could not keep her from her fateful flight on a rain-swept, windy night. It all brings to mind someone I knew who used to love my cheesecake.

Casablanca Cheesecake

Crust

2½ cups graham crackers or vanilla wafers, crushed

6 tablespoons melted butter

¼ cup sugar

½ teaspoon ground nutmeg

Filling

2½ pounds cream cheese (the real stuff; no substitutes), at room temperature

1¾ cups sugar

1 teaspoon pure vanilla extract

1½ teaspoons freshly grated lemon zest

¼ teaspoon salt

3 tablespoons unbleached white flour

5 whole eggs plus 2 egg yolks, at room temperature

½ cup heavy cream or evaporated milk

Topping

1½ cups sour cream

3 tablespoons sugar

½ teaspoon pure vanilla extract

Pinch of salt

Fresh fruit for garnish (optional)

To prepare the crust, mix all ingredients together in a small bowl with a fork. (An easy way to crush graham crackers is to double bag them in plastic and attack them with a rolling pin.) Using the flat bottom of a glass or measuring cup, press the crust mixture onto the bottom and partially up the sides of a 10-inch spring-form pan (lined with parchment, if you wish). Chill while preparing filling.

Preheat oven to 400°F. Make the filling: In a large mixing bowl, beat the cream cheese until fluffy. Add the sugar, vanilla, lemon zest, salt, and flour, and beat well. Add the eggs and yolks, *one at a time*, beating or whisking after each egg. Gently blend in the heavy cream. Pour into pan. Bake at 400°F for 10 minutes, reduce temperature to 225°F, and bake for an additional 70 to 80 minutes.

While the cheesecake is baking, whisk all ingredients for the topping together in a small bowl. Without jiggling the baking cake too much (no quick moves), gently spread the topping over the cheesecake. Increase oven temperature to 400°F and bake for another 5 to 7 minutes. To check for doneness, touch the top lightly with your finger. (Note the precise baking time for your next cheesecake adventure.)

Cool at room temperature and refrigerate for at least a few hours before serving. A garnish of fresh fruit always adds a classic touch.

Serves 1 to 10 and many memories.

It is only with the heart that one can see rightly;
what is essential is invisible to the eye.

—Antoine de Saint-Exupéry, *The Little Prince*

CHAPTER 4

Making Life a Picnic

FEEL-GOOD FEASTS AT NATURE'S TABLE

Bacchus, Bacchea, Bon . . . Vivant!

A cohort with his alter ego Dionysus, Bacchus was the ever-active god of wine and revelry and ecstatic liberation. Boy, it surely must have been tough keeping those mortals focused on their earthly obligations of pleasure! And pleasure was vital. As they saw it, when minds were flowing with the wine, a benevolent sense of peace infused social situations, and thus the well-being of civilization in general was promoted inadvertently. These gods were the picnic kings, ingraining in mortals the delights of dining outdoors and the heightened sensuality of taking food and refreshment under the heavens. In fact, the ancient Roman mid-March festival of Bacchanalia was a *compulsory* festival of drunken debauchery, dancing, carousing, and orgies.

Seriously folks, this was the good pagan's way of "going to church," loosely speaking, and giving the gods of gusto their due worship! The sacred sisters and high priestesses of the party, the *Bacchae* or *Maenades* ("frenzied ones"), were undoubtedly red-hot relatives of many present-day kitchen goddesses. Perhaps we now know the real cause of those passion-provoking bouts of spring fever—it's genetic!

With the resounding approval of the ancient gods and goddesses, permission to play is granted; our divine birthright ordains that we should revive the glorious and venerable institution of the picnic. Let the merrymaking, feasting, and festivities begin. According to ancient tradition, "making life a picnic" is not only expected, it is mandatory. The jamboree of life has begun!

Through the Vine, Toward Life!

The Brotherhood of the Knights of the Vine, a "medieval" association of individuals who share an appreciation for and an interest in the vines and wines of America, holds that wine is a gift from God . . . and a gift from nature. The knights have as their slogan: Water separates the people of the world; wine unites them. In our quest to honor and serve noble foods and wines at our tables, we are kindred spirits, we kitchen goddesses and the Gentleladies of the Vine.

The first wine knighthoods, known as *Conseils des échansons*—the councils of cup-bearers—were established in the thirteenth century when poisoning was an occupational hazard of royalty and their guests. The knights cultivated the vines, made and tasted the wines, and certified them "noble" before filling royal glasses. As noted by the Brotherhood, "Out of this evolved the etiquette of the table, the marriage of wine with food, and the tasting of the wine at the table before serving the guests."

Consider this item of interest: The tradition of toasting became popular in medieval days when slipping a Mickey meant dosing an adversary's drink with poison. When someone was handed a drink and a toast ensued, the toaster's life literally depended upon looking directly into the eyes of the toasting partner to intuit treachery or notice if there was any hesitation before the drink was sipped. From this practice, the toast, " To your health!" sprang forth. To your health indeed; it rather shades the popular toast, "To life!" in a different light.

Stop! Look! Listen!

The personalities and connotations of specific words often hold the ability to set our moods. Whether spoken, heard, or imagined, certain utterances send a prescribed notion drifting through the very essence of our being. What are your touchstone words and phrases? I've always enjoyed the feeling of *effortlessly*, *sweet potato*, *lubricious*, *relevant*, and *taffy apple pie*, but my favorite word of the day is actually a French word derived from the verb *flâner*, meaning to stroll: *flâneur*, a person who strolls about idly, as along the boulevards. Isn't that beautiful? *Je suis une flâneuse*: I am a person who loves to saunter about idly and blissfully.

Making life a picnic simply involves teaching ourselves to s-l-o-w down and learn to *Stop! Look!* and *Listen!* just as we were taught in kindergarten when crossing the street. *Stop!* Allow yourself more time each day to smell the cinnamon buns, to push the pause button on the wild chatter-dance in your mind, and to think before you speak—are these words "kind; necessary; helpful?" *Look!* Scrutinize the clouds for sundogs, gaze into the eyes of a baby or a feline, and practice the ancient divination arts of augury and aeromancy by recognizing intuitive messages received when watching birds or airplanes fly across the sky. *Listen!* Pay attention to a gurgling brook, to someone speaking ("keep me from that fatal habit of thinking I must say something on every occasion"), and to the subtle whispers in the sounds of words and how they make you *feel*—cinnamon . . . happy-thought-hopscotch . . . periwinkle . . . refreshing . . . embellish . . . cool . . . nonchalant . . . hummingbird-happiness . . . ecstasy . . . collective effervescence . . . insouciant . . . Tropical Bacchus Brew . . . Paradise State Fair Old-Time Lemonade . . . soothing . . . fun.

Tropical Bacchus Brew

¾ cup sugar

1 quart strong orange-spice tea

1 cup orange juice

1 can 7-Up

4 cups vodka

2 cups dark rum

1 teaspoon Angostura bitters

Large blocks of ice

2 oranges, cut into slices

Mint leaves

Dark cherries

Stir the sugar, tea, orange juice, and 7-Up together in a large punch bowl until the sugar dissolves. Add the vodka, rum, and bitters and stir well. Add the ice. Wedge a mint leaf into the center of each orange slice, and garnish the brew with oranges and cherries.

Makes enough tropical brew to arouse 4 to 6 bacchants and bacchantes to bliss.

Paradise State Fair Old-Time Lemonade

½ cup sugar

2 cups hot water

4 lemons

4 to 5 cups cold water

In a 2-quart pitcher, dissolve the sugar in hot water. Before cutting the lemons, roll them on the counter with the heel of your hand to release juices. Cut off the ends and slice each lemon into quarters. Squeeze the juice into the sugar water, and drop the rinds into the pitcher. Stir madly.

Top off the pitcher with cold water. Always serve the lemonade on ice with a lemon wedge floater or two. The lemonade will keep refrigerated for 24 hours with the lemon wedges in it. After that amount of time, remove the wedges to avoid bitterness.

Makes a 2-quart pitcher of lemonade, which provides 8 cups.

Never resist a generous impulse.

—Carushka

To help another, give them [sic] a drink from your cup.

—P. D. Cota-Robles

Relishing the Rituals of Womanhood

The mighty presence of alcohol in human history has been so pronounced that, as we've discovered in ancient cosmologies, patron gods—Dionysus and Bacchus—were assigned to oversee its function. Greek and Roman myth flows with references to wine, the nectar of mortals—an elixir of such stature that it was offered in sacrificial jubilation. The use of this joy juice spilled over, so to speak, into pre-Christian rituals before finding deep meaning in the stories of Jesus' first and last miracles—turning water into wine and turning wine into his own blood, respectively. The earth goddess Demeter was partial to *kykeon,* a blend of pennyroyal, barley meal, and water; the Egyptian goddess Isis taught her children the secrets of beer making.

It was believed that goddesses lurked among the grape vines, promising the mirth of inebriation to unsuspecting mortals. Though the earliest wine deities were female, laws were eventually passed in the dawning days of Rome forbidding women to partake of this libation. A sip of the stuff was punishable by death (and we think our drunk driving laws are harsh). Strega (witch), said to have been originally formulated by Italian witches, is revered as an alembic in purification diets; contemporary worshippers of the Hawaiian fire goddess, Pele, toss bottles of gin in the volcano to appease her.

Not all potent drinks are alcoholic; coffee, tea, and hot chocolate jump immediately to mind. At the start of the sixteenth century, after the Spaniards brought the precious substance, cocoa, back from Mexico, fasting Catholic clerics invented hot chocolate. As noted by Wolfgang Schivelbusch in *Tastes of Paradise*, "On the principle that liquids do not break fasts (*liquidum non frangit jejunum*), chocolate could serve as a nutritional substitute during fasting periods." Later, chocolate, still in a pourable form, was the staple at breakfasts of the aristocracy, served preferably in the boudoir or bed, to "mark the start of a day's carefully cultivated idleness."

With a drink in hand, I became a *real* woman when I was about seven years old. I had sneaked off with my cousin Theresa to a little café at her parents' beach club on the Gulf coast of Florida. On her cue, we naughtily ordered ice coffees. I remember pouring cream into the taboo ritualistic tumbler of ice coffee and, as if in a trance, watching it languidly swirl around the ice cubes. My life was about to change; we looked around to see if a grown up was spying on us and then secretly sipped our potions.

One of my most treasured rituals of womanhood today involves mixing up a pitcher of Bloody Marys on those luxurious Sunday mornings when I need to carefully cultivate my day's idleness. Somehow I have the idea that, if Catholic bishops saw chocolate as nutritious, I am home free with tomato juice, fruit juice (lemons!), and a liquor made from grain.

Sunday Bloody Mary Mix

I can (46 ounces) tomato juice

I teaspoon celery salt

¾ teaspoon black pepper

I tablespoon lemon juice

2 tablespoons Worcestershire sauce

2 teaspoons horseradish sauce

5 dashes Tabasco sauce (some like it hot!) or to taste

1½ to 2 shots of the best vodka you can afford per 8 ounces of mix

Old Bay seasoning to taste

Olives and celery, for garnish

Mix thoroughly in a large container. Store in a tightly covered container and always shake before using.

Mix with the quantity of vodka that you think a Bloody Mary should have in it, garnish with olives and celery, and don't make any plans to drive anywhere in the near future. R-e-l-a-x . . . it's Sunday!

Makes enough mix for 6 jumbo Bloody Marys.

An adventure is only an inconvenience rightly considered.
An inconvenience is only an adventure wrongly considered.

—G. K. Chesterton

To think of those we love is
a fine seasoning for joy.

—Molière

Dressed "To Die For"

W hat picnic would be complete without a superb salad and an equally fine salad dressing? So I called upon my cousin-in-law, Maria. She says of her recipe, "It is the smoothest dressing ever; salads beg for it—at least mine do—but then frankly, it's the only dressing recipe I know. I must say that this salad dressing really is to die for, and that's quite a challenge for any goddess who is supposed to be immortal. Plus, it's easy . . . and doesn't use any ingredients that you wouldn't always have around."

I must add this: The original version of this dressing was titled Tatty's Salad Dressing in honor of Maria's friend in the Twin Cities who created it. (This updated recipe is almost identical, but it has less oil, more garlic, and water-packed artichoke hearts.) Maria recalls that Tatty "liked to entertain, and obviously made a mean salad—or maybe turned very ordinary salads into masterpieces with her mean dressing." The dressing has a life of its own with many tales to tell, so let's mix it up and listen in.

Sassy Salad Dressing

¾ cup extra virgin olive oil

¼ cup red wine vinegar

1 tablespoon white wine

1 to 2 garlic cloves, mashed

1 teaspoon dried sweet basil

1 teaspoon paprika

1 jar (6 ounces) chopped artichoke hearts with marinade

½ teaspoon dried thyme

Salt and freshly milled black pepper to taste

Put all ingredients in a shaker and rock and roll. Feel free to use artichoke hearts packed in water if you want to avoid the oil.

Makes 1½ cups.

The secret of success is making your vocation your vacation.

—Mark Twain

Between living and dreaming
there is a third thing . . .
Guess it!

—Antonio Machado

Soul Salad Blessing

When the idea of this cookbook first alighted in my mind and I was beseeching family and friends to share their favorite foods, my sister Kate and her hubby, Jeff, sprang forth with a suggestion for a meal that included this recipe for spinach salad. With their recipes they shared this. "Before beginning a meal, we bless our food, each person taking his/her turn to celebrate the unique way this nourishment will have expression in the given moment. Every meal is different, even if it resembles another, and should be honored for offering our bodies renewal and hope. Our relationship with food reflects our loving exchange with life and others, and vice versa. Blessing what we eat is a reminder of this, promoting optimum vitality of spirit." To this insight Kate added, "If something appeals to the palate and imagination of children, then it's got to be good for the soul."

This salad is light and flavorful, the color stimulating. My daughter loves to pick the mandarins out to pop in her mouth; it obviously has her blessing.

Mandarin Spinach Salad

Dressing

¼ cup canola oil

1 tablespoon grated Parmesan cheese

2 tablespoons Dijon-style mustard

1 teaspoon sugar

1 teaspoon Worcestershire sauce

Juice of 1 large lemon

1 teaspoon minced garlic

1 teaspoon black pepper

¼ teaspoon salt

1 raw egg or equivalent egg substitute (optional)

½ teaspoon poppy seeds (optional)

❧

1 bunch (8 to 10 ounces), spinach leaves rinsed and stems removed

2 hard-boiled eggs, cooled and chopped

3 to 4 slices bacon, cooked, drained, and crumbled

1 can (11 ounces) mandarin orange sections, drained and cut into halves

Combine the oil, cheese, mustard, sugar, Worcestershire, lemon juice, garlic, pepper, salt, and egg (if using) in a blender. Combine until smooth. Add poppy seeds if desired. Place the spinach in a chilled bowl. Drizzle the dressing over the spinach and toss gently. Immediately before serving, add the chopped eggs, bacon, and mandarin oranges and jostle a touch.

Serves 4.

A la Goddess

* Cantaloupes in season provide a delightful alternative to mandarin slices and the colorful pizazz of the salad is also preserved.

There are two kinds of people on earth today,
just two kinds of people on earth . . .
the people who lift and the people who lean.

—Ella Walker Wilcox

A German Gem from Bonnie's

*A*nother soul pleaser, this Eurocousin of our traditional needs-to-be-refrigerated picnic fare offers that type of goose-bump comfort that only warm, creamy, sensually spiced foods provide. This potato salad wins applause for cooler evening picnic fare or as a complementary dish during spring or fall outdoor festivities to ward off any encroaching chill. This particular recipe is a mirrored image (I added a few magic touches) of the bestseller at Bonnie's Restaurant on Aspen Mountain in Aspen, Colorado, known worldwide for its German-Austrian good ol' homemade cuisine (more infamously known as the site of Ivana Trump and Marla Maple's ungoddesslike cat fight).

This German potato salad, the handmade apple strudel, and Missen's lemon bars (see page 132) were my staple, double-dessert lunch for the years I baked for Bonnie. (Write and trade your best recipe, and I'll send you the authentic Aspen Mountain Golden Apple Strudel recipe!) Fortunately, to burn off some of these delicious calories, the only way down the mountain was to ski.

Hot German Potato Salad

4 to 5 slices bacon, diced

½ cup chopped onion

¼ cup brown sugar

1½ teaspoons salt

½ teaspoon black pepper

2 tablespoons unbleached white flour

1 egg

¼ cup apple cider vinegar

Juice of 1 large lemon

1 cup warm water

1 chicken bouillon cube, mashed with fork

2 tablespoons minced fresh parsley

1 teaspoon celery or caraway seed, your choice

6 potatoes, boiled in their skins, peeled, sliced and kept warm

Paprika for garnish

In a large skillet, fry the diced bacon until it is brown. Remove bacon and drain off excess fat, reserving 2 to 3 tablespoons in the pan. Sauté the onion with sugar, salt, and pepper until onion is translucent. Blend in the flour.

In a separate bowl, beat the egg with vinegar, lemon juice, water, and bouillon cube. Gradually add this to the mixture in the pan and stir. Sprinkle in parsley and either celery or caraway seeds. Cook over low heat until thick. Add the bacon and stir. Pour the hot dressing over hot, sliced potatoes and toss lightly. This potato salad should be kept in a metal bowl or pan and is always served warm.

Serves 6 to 8.

A la Goddess

*The secret to handling hot potatoes is to run them under cool water while you peel them quickly with a dull knife; the skin should slide right off.

There is a charm in improvised eating
which a regular meal lacks . . .
a glamour never to be recaptured.

—Graham Greene

Some Trends Are Worth Trying

*T*his recipe holds the award for being the trendiest one in my repertoire. Anything Thai is hot—in food or travel—and turkey has been a low-fat, trendy tidbit for a while now. There is a reason for such popularity: "It does a body good." Inspired by a recipe created by my friend Susan, the Thai Turkey Picnic Wrap's first incarnation was as a pasta salad. Though absolutely fabulous, we couldn't get it to travel well to the beach. Hence the change.

Another vital reason we created a less complicated, hands-on picnic vittle is simply this: Susan's husband Fred is a master brewer for a very popular microbrewery in Northern California. When Susan, Fred, and their minihockey team consisting of Philip, Ian, and Scarlet (the goalie) arrive, we barely have enough hands to haul cases of ice-cold ale to the feast. So often, by the time we kick into food-prep mode, the outdoor kitchen goddesses have lost their lust for the barbie and are reclining under a shady tree savoring the fruits—or let's say the *grains*, hops, wheat, and barley—of Fred's loving labor. Wrap in one hand, brewski in another—it's instant picnic time!

Thai Turkey Picnic Wraps

½ cup tamari or soy sauce

4 tablespoons rice vinegar

2 teaspoons powdered sugar

3 teaspoons cornstarch

1 Anaheim chili, seeded and finely minced

2 tablespoons oil

½ turkey breast (approximately 2½ pounds), boned and skinned and diced

4 cloves garlic, finely minced

1 large Bermuda onion, thinly sliced

1 cup fresh basil, chopped

1 tablespoon fresh mint, chopped

1 medium carrot

1 small (8-ounce) jicama

Four 9-inch flour tortillas, flatbread, or nan bread (*experiment!*)

Mix the tamari, vinegar, sugar, and cornstarch together. Add chili and set aside.

Heat 2 tablespoons of the oil in a wok over high heat. Add the turkey and cook for 1 minute. Add garlic and cook about 4 minutes, until meat is no longer pink. Remove turkey from wok and keep warm.

Heat another tablespoon of oil in wok and add onion. Cook, covered, for 2 minutes. Return the turkey and juices to the wok, add tamari mixture, and stir until the sauce begins to thicken. Turn off heat, add basil and mint, and cook covered for 1 minute. Remove from wok, and store in a proper container for transportation. Refrigerate if it will not be eaten within an hour or two.

Peel and julienne or coarsely grate the carrot and jicama and store in a separate containers. When ready to serve, spoon the turkey mixture onto the tortillas or bread, garnish with carrots and jicama, and wrap it up.

Makes 4 wraps.

A la Goddess

* If you want your wrap to be hot, and you have access to a grill, wrap the "wrap" in tinfoil and heat on the grill for 5 minutes before eating.

* If you prefer to remain un-"wrapped," this sauce recipe is also remarkably compatible with pasta and chicken. The goddess who gave me the recipe suggests using 4 chicken breasts and increasing sauce ingredients by one-half. Then toss an extra tablespoon *each* of soy sauce, vinegar, and oil with a head of thinly sliced Napa cabbage and a few green onions with the whites and one-half of the greens finely chopped. Cook a pound of pasta of your choice (may we suggest capellini or Chinese noodles?), rinse with cold water, and toss with 1 tablespoon oil. Mix everything together and refrigerate until picnic time. Serves up to 4.

**If you obey all the rules,
you miss all the fun.**

—Katherine Hepburn

A Rainbow of Tastes

*B*y now I hope you have noticed how the taste of food is enhanced when taken outside. The delights of dining under the heavens outweigh the added inspiration necessary to plan and prepare food that is safe to eat when subjected to an assortment of temperature changes, holds its flavor, and is travel friendly. These pastoral feel-good feasts serve to pull us out of the ordinary, mundane patterns of cooking and consuming. Simply taking a different path from the kitchen to a novel dining area—a picnic table or blanket—is refreshing.

If we were all so lucky to experience frequent timeouts on a tropical island, maybe we'd picnic more. The beach sunsets, perfectly refreshing trade winds, and prismatic rainbows beg to be celebrated with a scrumptious outdoor meal topped by a piña colada or bottle of wine. In honor of Iris, the indwelling goddess spirit of the rainbow—that cosmic bridge between heaven and earth—I share one of my best-kept, most colorful secrets.

Island Casserole

1 cup medium-grain rice

1 teaspoon pure vanilla extract, divided

3 tablespoons unsweetened coconut milk, divided

¾ pound fresh ahi or mahimahi, lightly cooked, and cut into ½-inch pieces

1¾ cups crushed pineapple in natural juices

1 teaspoon curry powder

¾ teaspoon saffron, crushed

½ teaspoon Old Bay seasoning

¼ teaspoon minced garlic (optional)

Salt to taste

1 can (14 ounces) water-packed artichoke hearts, drained

½ cup Monterey Jack cheese, grated

Paprika

Prepare rice according to package instructions, adding ¼ teaspoon of the vanilla and 1 tablespoon of the coconut milk to the water as it cooks. Dress the fish with a few dashes of your favorite seasonings (I like Old Bay) and lightly sear, broil, or grill it.

Heat oven to 325°F. In a large bowl, combine cooked rice with the pineapple and its juice, the remaining 2 tablespoons coconut milk and ¾ teaspoon vanilla, curry powder, saffron, Old Bay seasoning, and garlic if desired, and mix well. Season with a few dashes of salt. Tenderly stir in prepared fish, and spoon mixture into a 2-quart casserole or baking dish. Top with artichoke hearts, sprinkle with cheese, and garnish with a few good shakes of paprika. Bake, uncovered, for 20 to 25 minutes.

Serves 4.

A la Goddess

* Feel free to explore other variations of taste and seasonings if you wish. Substitute other lightly cooked seafood—scallops, shrimp, langoustines, even canned white albacore tuna—if you prefer.

* Serve with fresh tropical fruit and Hawaiian Sweet Potato Bread (page 40). Put on your hula skirts, fill your cups to overflowing with Tropical Bacchus Brew (page 116) and drift away with the tastes of Paradise.

The Perfect Picnic Dessert

Missen, Bonnie's intrepidly bright and brilliant daughter (and my "most fun" friend for the years I worked at Bonnie's restaurant) graced me with this recipe, handwritten, for my twenty-fifth birthday. We always called her "Missen—as in gone." Growing up in one of America's premier ski resorts, she was impossible to keep up with when she was on skis. I hear Miss is back in Aspen, stirring up a culinary career of her own. With her mother as her mentor, I can only imagine that Missen is hot on my heels of holding the claim to the being the best strudel-rolling fräulein in Bonnie's history.

Missen's Lemon Bars

Crust

2 cups unbleached white flour

½ cup sugar

I cup butter, at room temperature

Lemon Filling

1½ cups sugar

¼ cup unbleached white flour

Juice and finely grated rind of 3 lemons

I teaspoon baking powder

3 eggs

Powdered sugar, for decoration

Preheat oven to 350°F. Mix crust ingredients together and press into a greased, 9-by-13-by-2-inch glass baking dish. Bake for 10 to 15 minutes. Cool for 10 minutes before adding filling.

While crust is cooling, make the filling. Mix all ingredients together and pour over the cooled crust. Bake for 20 to 30 minutes. Sprinkle powdered sugar on top after lemon bars have cooled (at least 15 minutes) and cut while in the pan.

Makes 18 bars.

Taking a Byte of Virtual Cake

If you ever feel like your apron strings are starting to strangle you and your epicurean imagination is beginning to wilt like yesterday's lettuce in the Arizona sun, go surfing. Forgo the fridge, visit **www.kingarthurflour.com,** and try the recipe for the Lazy Daisy Cake. Or look for some cooking ideas at **www.kitchenlink.com, www.culinarycafe.com,** or **www.bpe.com,** San Francisco food enthusiast Sally Bernstein's home page. And my latest creation **www.foodthatrocks.com** simply rocks!

Craving chocolate? Hop over to **www.chocolocate.com** or **www.godiva.com.** When you're ready to repent, click on **www.ediet.com** or **www.fatfree.com.** Or maybe you just want to fall back into the safety net of virtual macaroni and cheese and other comfort food recipes at **www.kraftfoods.com**, **www.landolakes.com**, and **www.cambellsoups.com**.

Don't stop yet: **www.epicurious.com** has more than six thousand recipes at your fingertips, **www.foodchannel.com** links you to contests, games, and restaurant reviews, and **www.foodtv.com** will lure you with a line-up of the latest and greatest cooking shows.

After all this cyberspice, you just may be ready to return to your kitchen and don the apron. After all, a good day of surfing takes a lot of energy, and by now, your virtual appetite is poised to raid a bona fide **www.refrigerator.com**.

Life itself is the proper binge.

—Julia Child

Take a "Day On"

*I*f you're feeling overwhelmed by responsibility, work, or even the demands of a hungry family, rather than take a day off, why not take a "day *on?*" Envelop yourself in activities that refresh and pleasure you. Instead of tuning things *out*, turn your senses *on*. Instead of a *sick* day, take a *well* day. If you are too uninspired to cook, skip a meal and eat fresh fruit, carrots, and yogurt instead (no one will starve), or entice someone to invite you to dinner (just use your imagination!).

A "day on" simply involves doing what you love to do; this may take a bit of planning, especially if you have children (and the often mundane demands of their schedules) to tend to, but by allowing yourself a flip-flop view of the day-to-day ordinary, life has a way of presenting you the extraordinary. As Sark suggests, "Let pleasure find you." Choose your muse . . .

My "day on" will include:

1.

2.

3.

Ten thousand flowers in spring, the moon in autumn,
a cool breeze in summer, snow in winter.
If your mind isn't clouded by unnecessary things,
this is the best season of your life.

—Wu-men

Have Brownies, Will Climb

There is no doubt in my mind that, if the wild and unapproachable Artemis were to transform herself into a modern-day goddess, her name would be Charlotte Fox. Instead of quiver and arrows, she would sport a climbing harness and cleats, and rather than rule the forests and woods, she would be found working her magic on the mountaintops she so holds as sacred. When my friend Charlotte's not climbing, she's probably hiking, mountain biking, or ski patrolling. Considering the amount of time she spends outdoors, she has honorarily reached the ranks of a feral picnic goddess—we'll probably never see her in a kitchen.

If you ask her to share her best cooking advice, she'll recommend, "Buy from a professional." Her best technical tip: "Flip through Margie's cookbook." I hear she has a bread machine, but I can't say if she's ever fired it up. She simply advises, "Go good, healthy, and easy." Artemis would glow with pride.

If secrets are being told—and I guess they are—we'd know that, instead of sustaining her energy with ambrosia, this unassuming wild woman would be carbing up on one of her favorite delicacies, fudge brownies—"the essence of wantonness." I'm sure these brownies will make it to the picnic with Charlotte; maybe even to the top of her next mountain.

Magic Double-Fudge Brownies

1 pound (2 cups) butter

8 ounces unsweetened chocolate

4 cups sugar

8 eggs

2 teaspoons pure vanilla extract

¾ teaspoon salt

2¼ cups unbleached white flour

2 cups semisweet chocolate chips

1 cup chopped walnuts, or more (optional)

Slowly melt the butter and chocolate together on low, low, low heat in a very large, heavy saucepan. While they are melting, grease and flour a large sheet or jelly-roll pan or two 9-by-13-by-2-inch pans (a commercial 12-by-17-inch "half flat" is the ideal size). Stir the melted chocolate and butter together, add the sugar, and mix well with a wooden spoon. Allow this chocolate syrup to remain on the stove for about 5 minutes, until the sugar melts.

Preheat the oven to 325°F. In a separate, large bowl (not any smaller than 8 quarts), beat the eggs, vanilla, and salt together. While stirring (have someone help you if possible), add the chocolate syrup to the egg mixture; stir until it becomes shiny.

Gently stir in flour, taking care not to create too many bubbles. Add the chocolate chips and walnuts (or toss a few handfuls of nuts on top of the batter in the pans if that is what you prefer). Pour into pan or pans. Bake for 25 to 28 minutes, no more. You will either have to trust this recipe or rely on your instinct to tell if brownies are done.

Makes forty-eight 2-inch square brownies.

It is impossible to live a pleasant life
without living wisely and well and justly, and
it is impossible to live wisely and well and justly
without living a pleasant life.

—Epicurus

The Perfect Picnic Partner

*I*f the phone messages you had left with your life-in-the-fast-lane friends had gone unanswered and you were looking for a fun, last-minute picnic partner, you would call Paula Pensiero. A rare, paradoxical rainbow of a woman, she is simultaneously self-confident and naive, calm and energized, cultured and ferociously feral. She's wise, worldly, and instantly likeable—Paula simply owns the gift of bringing out the best in people. Whether skiing (she's a former member of the U.S. National Championship Sierra Nevada College ski team), running a premier snowcat ski resort (www.baldface.net), conversing with a six-year-old, or dancing in a minidress at a deck party, this girl is making life a picnic.

Paula's picnics are always minimanifestations of her life: the refreshments flow, the bread is homemade, the energy gentle and glowing, and the conversation eclectic and natural—never forced. And because she takes pleasure in creating desserts that are as multifaceted as she is, my guess is the picnic would be crowned with one of her whimsical pies.

Pepper-Peach Rainbow Pie

One 9-inch pie crust (see page 104 for recipe)

Filling

3 McIntosh or Golden Delicious apples

4 big peaches

1 cup dark cherries, pitted (thawed if frozen

⅔ cup raw sugar

2 tablespoons unbleached white flour

2 tablespoons quick-cooking tapioca

1 teaspoon ground cinnamon

1 teaspoon ground nutmeg

2 teaspoons lemon juice

1 teaspoon pure vanilla extract (optional)

Pinch of salt

Pinch of pepper (for good luck!)

Topping

¼ cup unbleached white flour

¼ cup raw sugar

¾ teaspoon ground cinnamon

3 tablespoons chilled butter

Make the pie dough first. Roll it to a ⅛-inch thickness and line a deep 9-inch pie dish. Cover with plastic wrap and refrigerate.

Preheat oven to 400°F. Peel, core, and slice apples. Halve the peaches, remove the pits and slice. Toss the apples, peaches, cherries, sugar, flour, tapioca, spices, lemon juice, optional vanilla, and salt together delicately. Pour mixture into pie shell, gently press into shape, and consecrate with a few shakes of pepper on top.

Mix the topping ingredients together, using a fork to cut in the chilled butter until the mixture takes on a crumbly texture. Sprinkle the topping over the rainbow mixture. Bake at 400°F for 10 minutes. Reduce heat to 350°F and bake for 50 more minutes, or until pie is a desired golden brown.

Serves 8.

Get your facts first, and then you can
distort them as much as you please.

—Mark Twain

Do Your Thing Your Way

*I*mpromptu picnicking is one of the most redeeming wonders of this harried, hurried world. To disengage ourselves from the phone, the fax, and
the computer, and the demands of a bottomless sink of dishes, emanci-
pates the spirit. Simply by stepping outdoors to savor a meal while surrounded by fresh
breezes, wood nymphs, beach spirits, or garden sprites gives us permission to redefine
ourselves as libertines, sensualists, and voluptuaries. We launch into a free flight from
obligation into the embrace of sybarism . . . ah-h-h-h-h.

The moment the spirit moves me, or a friend says, "Let's have a picnic!" I glance
around the kitchen and take a quick mental inventory of ingredients at my fingertips—
shopping for an impromptu fling is never allowed. Then I begin to visualize my feast.
Creating dishes by vibration with no real road map, improvising with the treasures I find
in cubbies, fridge, or cabinets, supplies an "ooh-ah" feeling of carefree accomplishment.

The following recipe provides a gentle introduction to Vibration Cooking 101.
When tossing the crisp together, I favor grouping my fruits, distinguishing those that
grow on trees or bushes from the hard-stoned varieties, such as apricots, cherries,
peaches, and plums.

Wild Card Crisp

Filling

8 to 9 cups fruit, sliced if necessary
(avoid tropical and citrus fruit)

½ cup brown sugar

¼ cup white sugar

¼ cup unbleached white flour

2 tablespoons quick-cooking tapioca

1 tablespoon fresh lemon juice

2 teaspoons ground cinnamon

1 teaspoon ground nutmeg

Topping

1½ cups brown sugar

1½ cup rolled oats

1 cup unbleached white flour

¾ cup butter, chilled and cut into pieces

2 teaspoons ground cinnamon

½ teaspoon ground nutmeg

Preheat oven to 350°F and grease a large (15-by-10-by-2½-inch) baking pan. Toss the filling ingredients together in a large bowl and spoon into the pan.

To make the topping, mix sugar, oats, and flour, and, with a large fork, cut in the butter, then blend in the spices.. Sprinkle the topping over the fruit mixture and bake, uncovered, for 50 minutes to an hour. (Cover the pan with tinfoil if, toward the end of the baking time, the top of the crisp begins to brown too much.) Serves 12.

And when I cook, I never measure or weigh anything. I cook by vibration . . .
Some of the recipes that people gave me list the amounts,
but for my part, I just do it by vibration. . . . Do your thing your way.

—Verta Mae, *Vibration Cooking*

Goddess! I have beheld those eyes before
And their eternal calm, and all that face,
Or I have dream'd?

—John Keats

A Midnight Dream Picnic

The fountains of Rome, with their eternal rivers glistening in the moonlight, create a supernal nocturne for a midnight picnic. Every polished stone, chiseled by a masterful artist and caressed by a substance so powerful it is called "the source of life," holds a rich history. The rambling subtle rhythm of the water music can ring wild in the soul and heart. These are the baths of the goddess.

When I first visited the Eternal City, a sense of awe, wonder, and déjà vu swirling about me—I had the clearest feeling of reincarnation I've ever known. My footsteps echoed as I walked the narrow cobblestone streets to the piazza; ancient footprints were everywhere. I recall, while exploring the piazzas one evening, slipping into a delicious fantasy . . .

My name is Avallonia de Medici, a maiden fair and felicitous, intentionally lost on the baroque-frosted streets of Rome hundreds of years ago. When I serendipitously come upon the Piazza Navona, I am stunned by the extraordinary water pageantry of Gianlorenzo Bernini's newly sculpted *Fountain of the Four Rivers*. Wistfully, I sit where the mist touches my face.

A boy—he calls himself Benedetto—is also sitting on the fountain's edge, strumming a melancholy guitar and singing ballads to a girl he vowed to love for eternity. He says she is gone, but her spirit rises in the water's mist, and the touch of that dew soothes his fevered longings. He offers me a plate of oranges. As I taste the sweetness of the orange, I am suddenly enchanted by the sight of the incandescent moon shimmering through the veiled mist, and I swear I hear a woman laughing, laughing . . .

Zapped back to my body by the rumblings in a hungry tummy, I sat near a cool fountain, sliced several zesty oranges, and sprinkled them with the sweet cherry liqueur in my backpack. The vision had turned my attention to the works of Bernini, all of which seemed so familiar. Relaxing in the embrace of the city's starlight, I recalled his controversial masterpiece, the *Ecstasy of Santa Teresa*, that I had seen earlier in the day.

Applauding critics—Camilla Paglia among them—claim that Saint Teresa is depicted weightless and swooning at the height of orgasmic release; defenders of the Holy Faith say she is in the overwhelming, billowy throes of the touch of God. In her own words Teresa exclaimed, "it was the sweetest caressing of the soul . . . ." Goddess to goddess, I could only imagine she would feel the same about *Le Arance Benedette* and the repast and pleasure they give when enjoyed near the fountains of Rome . . . at night.

Le Arance Benedette
(Blessed Oranges)

3 large, perfectly ripe Maltese (blood) oranges

Luxardo maraschino liqueur

A water fountain in Rome

Peel and slice the oranges, through the axis, into ¼-inch-thick wheels. Arrange on a beautiful large plate—crystal is always nice. Drizzle an abundant amount (at least one cup) of maraschino liqueur over the orange slices. Using fingers, feed them to a friend, preferably by a water fountain in Rome.

Serves 2.

A LA GODDESS

* The tart cherry taste of the liqueur married with the sweet juice of the orange tickles the palate with orgiastic bursts of flavor. If you cannot find Maltese oranges, regular navels will suffice. If you cannot find a fountain, perhaps a mountain stream, a cool swimming pool on a warm night, a Jacuzzi on a cool night, a large bathtub, or a balmy beach may flavor the fantasy.

CHAPTER 5

Vestal Pleasures

FOOD FOR
SAVORING
SOLITUDE

I know exactly what I'm doing darling;
you don't have to hope that I do.

—Gloria Swanson

We all partake in beloved indulgences when we are alone. These are the comforting culinary creations that ground us, refresh our souls, and tickle our taste buds. Who but a sibling or a soulmate would honestly and eagerly partake of precious closet delicacies such as grilled peanut butter and mayonnaise sandwiches, chocolate chip omelets, Cream of Wheat with ice cream, or British chip butties—french fry sandwiches? With whom can one share in the savory satisfaction of S & W dark red kidney beans doused with Tabasco sauce and a good sprinkling of Old Bay seasoning and eaten right out of the can? We each have our unique and secret food pleasures to indulge in when solo.

The Roman goddess Vesta, and her Greek soul sister Hestia, lived contented, illumined lives far from society's grip. Revered as the goddesses of the hearth and temple—both places of centered, sacred repose—they were esteemed as wise women, keepers of peace and serenity. In this light, eating alone can also provide a succulent time of regeneration, relaxation, and unabashed, guilt-free liberty to eat anything you want. The absence of conversation is in itself refreshing, particularly if you have little ones. The restorative, orgasmic lack of obligation, the quiet, the ability to dream one's dreams, the total tranquil absorption of the moment—these are the goddess-given gifts bestowed when we take a seat closest to Vesta's hearth.

While serenely sauntering through this chapter, you have full license to don your frightful avocado-honey-oatmeal pore-reducing moisture mask, pour yourself a flute of

Champagne, and eat the fruits of your labor-free labor while reclining in the style of a self-indulgent Roman goddess. You will emerge with the glowing fervor of delightful satisfaction.

Immortal Morsels from Flavorful Pages

Cakes and Ale by W. Somerset Maugham

The Art of Eating by M. F. K. Fisher

How to Be a Domestic Goddess: Baking and the Art of Comfort Cooking by Nigella Lawson

True Success by Tom Morris

Illusions by Richard Bach

In the Kitchen with Rosie by Rosie Daley

Practical Magic by Alice Hoffman

Jambalaya by Luisah Teish

The Joy of Cooking by Irma von Starkloff Rombauer

Food Men Love by Margie Lapanja

Wild Women in the Kitchen from the Wild Women Association

The Women's Encyclopedia of Myths and Secrets by Barbara G. Walker

The Master and Margarita by Mikhail Bulgakov

The Black Family Reunion Cookbook from the National Council of Negro Women

Succulent Wild Woman by Sark

The Physiology of Taste by Brillat-Savarin, translated by M. F. K. Fisher

To love oneself is the beginning of a life-long romance.

—Oscar Wilde

Eat Dessert First

To consecrate this sanctuary of sweet solitude fittingly, let us sequester our-selves and first share in a sinfully sensational oblation of what I call the Holy Trinity Ultra-indulgence: cream puffs oozing with a heavenly choco-late mousse and smothered in the most decadent chocolate sauce known to civilization.

Dream Puffs

¼ cup water	¼ cup unbleached white flour
2 tablespoons butter	I egg
Pinch of salt	

Preheat oven to 400°F and line a baking sheet with parchment. In a heavy saucepan with a sturdy handle, bring water, butter, and salt to a brisk boil. Keep the pan on the heat and add the flour *all at once*. Hold the handle tightly and stir vigorously with a strong wooden spoon until the mixture leaves the sides of the pan and forms a ball around the spoon. Add egg, and beat the mixture each time until smooth and glossy.

Drop by whopping tablespoons to form one large or two small puffs on the prepared pan. Bake immediately at 400°F for 10 minutes. *Without opening the door to peek,* reduce heat to 350°F and bake for 20 to 25 minutes longer. Gently remove puff(s) from the oven and delicately pierce in three places with a knife, allowing steam to escape, thus avoiding collapse. Allow to cool in the open air.

When cooled, slice the top(s) off and fill with Chocolate Rum Mousse, ice cream, whipped cream, or whatever your soul desires. Replace the sliced-off lid(s) and drizzle with Hot Fudge Sauce. Do a little dance and satisfy your soul!

Serves 1.

A la Goddess

*This recipe can be doubled or even quadrupled—but be sure that you add the eggs one at a time.

∽

Chocolate Rum Mousse

1 cup Hershey's chocolate chips	2 cups whipping cream, unwhipped
4 eggs, separated	¾ cup sugar
2 shots (3 ounces) rum	

Melt the chocolate chips in a double boiler, a pan floating in a water bath, or easier still, the microwave. In a large (stainless steel if you have one) bowl, whisk the egg yolks until a ribbon forms. Patiently add chocolate *a little at a time.*

Add rum to the chocolate mixture.

In a medium bowl, whip egg whites until stiff peaks form. Set aside. Whip the cream and sugar together in a large bowl until fluffy. Gently fold in chocolate mixture, and fold in whipped egg whites.

Serves 6—that's 5 for the future and 1 right now!

A la Goddess

* There are many ways to serve this luscious mousse:

    If using as Dream Puff filling, dollop to full capacity and replace the lid of the puff
    Pour into a beautiful large glass bowl
    Pour into 6-ounce serving glasses to make individual portions

* File this spirited equation for the future: 1 *shot* or *jigger* of liquor equals 1½ fluid ounces, which equals 3 tablespoons. A *pony* equals ½ fluid ounce or 1 tablespoon.

∽

Hot 'n' Creamy Fudge Sauce

8 ounces unsweetened chocolate

1 pound butter

7 cups powdered sugar

3 cups heavy cream, unwhipped

In a large, heavy saucepan over barely any heat (this takes patience, but don't blow it), melt chocolate and butter until smooth. Alternately whisk in powdered sugar and cream, and stir until shiny and smooth. Leave on low heat for 15 minutes, taking care *not to boil*. Stir occasionally.

Serve with Dream Puffs, ice cream, or favorite body parts. (C'mon now, I was only thinking fingers; this is a chapter about eating alone, remember?)

Makes approximately 1½ quarts of fudge.

A la Goddess

*Yes, this recipe makes a lot of fudge. The fudge keeps nicely when refrigerated and can be reheated in the microwave or in a water bath on the stove. Or share the spirit by pouring some homemade Hot 'n' Creamy Fudge Sauce in a decorative jar— it makes a bewitchingly unforgettable gift.

The Ancient Art of Bathing Cuisine

Eating in the bathtub is a luxurious, sybaritic delight. I recommend limiting your menu selection to an array of ripe fruit, simple finger foods, a flute of bubbly mineral water, or a glass of cheer. The preparation of the bath is also essential to heighten the value of the experience. To draw a delicious bath, light a scented candle, run the water to a desired temperature, and add a handful of your favorite bath salts. A tubful of abundant, silky bubbles is a requirement, so add a foaming agent. (My favorite bubble bath is Palmolive dishwashing soap for sensitive skin—the best!) As your bath foams, set the ambience with music and prepare your feast. When you have the mood and food in flow, slip into the arms of luxury and melt into a state of sensual bliss. Ah-h-h-h.

A particularly good bath is what I call the Attraction Bath, a bath in which to draw upon subconscious desires and nourish them with powerful and lucid meditation and visualization.

Clean your tub with sea salt, and visualize all negativity in the immediate moment flowing down the drain. Light a yellow candle (or candles) for attraction and prepare the tub with bubbles and bath salts. As you undress, begin to focus upon what you wish to manifest. (Please, be certain that this is a true—not a fleeting—soul-felt desire before proceeding.)

Either make a sachet of one handful each of dried yarrow flowers, parsley, and chamomile to steep in the tub, or toss a handful of each of these herbs into the water. Bathe with honey. As you bathe, clear your thoughts and look ahead energetically—*feel* your future. Then, when you are focused and clear, recite the following:

> *Earth, water, wind, and fire,*
> *Within my heart burns this desire,*
> *and so I pledge unto myself,*
> *Love, power, wealth, and health.*
> *Bless me with _____ or better.*

Trust that your request was received—beyond and within. Envision yourself basking in the *energy* of your creation . . . and then *release the outcome.* As you step out of the Attraction Bath, always remember to say "Thank you."

You will do foolish things,
but do them with enthusiasm.

—Colette

She Wrote the Book
on Playing Hard to Get

Mythological rumors circulate that Vesta, goddess of the hearth and home, could have had Apollo, the fleet-footed athlete and first victor in the Olympic Games, as her husband, but she refused. She preferred, instead, to remain a virgin and surround herself with priestesses of the same persuasion. The ancient Roman version of Greta Garbo, Vesta moved about, veiled in mystery, choosing to take no part in love or war.

Even when Dionysus, the god of wine, stole her spot on Mount Olympus, she simply resigned herself to being an absentee goddess and kept the fires burning elsewhere with her six girlfriends. Of course, Aphrodite, the busy goddess of love, couldn't understand this aloof air of contentment. After not being able to "awaken a pleasant yearning" in Vesta, ol' Aphrodite started stirring it up.

She made Apollo fall in love with this cool-as-a-cucumber goddess. Regardless of the swooning, honey-noted love songs that dripped from his golden lyre, her virgin ears were deaf to his musical invitation. In the ultimate game of "hard to get," Vesta took her torch—obviously *not* carried for Apollo—jumped on her favored ass which she had decorated with garlands of violets and loaves of bread, and trotted off to a temple in Rome.

Meanwhile, dejected Apollo, god of prophecy, foresaw a plan in which his twin sister Artemis would get Vesta drunk on his home-brew so the spirit-enflamed virgin goddess would hop on her donkey and gallop back to Mount Olympus for a little hanky panky. In honor of the tale, I offer two potent potions; had Apollo possessed the recipe for Russian Huntress, christened of course in the honor of his wild, hunt-happy sister, Vesta might have no longer been a virgin. Until he slips her a Mickey, her sacred fire continues to burn alone.

Home-brew "Kahlua"

4 cups water

5 cups sugar

1 jar (2 ounces) instant coffee
(Yuban works well)

4 cups vodka

1 large vanilla bean, cut into pieces
or 3 tablespoons pure vanilla extract

In a large heavy saucepan, bring water to a boil; add sugar and coffee and leave over heat for 3 to 4 minutes more. Remove from heat and let cool *completely*.

When mixture has cooled, add vodka and vanilla. Pour into a glass 1-gallon container and let season for at least three weeks to a month, shaking once a day. (However, I must note that Apollo has since confessed he can rarely wait a month before sampling it—and it serves its divine purpose at any point in the concocting process.) Strain the elixir into decorative decanter and enjoy as you please.

Makes ½ gallon of homebrew.

Russian Huntress

Crushed ice

2½ shots Home-brew "Kahlua"

1 to 1½ shots vodka

Half-and-half to top the glass

Approximately ¼ shot Galliano liqueur

Fill a highball glass almost to the top with crushed ice. Pour in Home-brew Kahlua, vodka, and enough half-and-half to almost top the glass. Pour in the Galliano float and stir. Serve with care; guaranteed to incite the wild woman in one female.

Makes 1 drink.

I mix everything I can.
We live in an era of contrasts,
everything is fast and mixed,
like fast food and gourmet meals.
I translate that . . .

—Gianni Versace

For wisdom moves more easily than motion itself;
she is so pure she pervades and permeates all things.

—Wisdom 7:24

The Diet Deity

When I was an untamed wildflower of a teenager, my mother and I held wanton late-night binge rituals consuming Ritz crackers slathered with cream cheese (there was no such thing as fat-free cream cheese then) and homemade strawberry jam. These ambrosial appetizers were the most exquisite Vestal pleasure shared in a most clandestine fashion. (As Mom says with a gleam in her eye, "They *still* are.") Hard to hide, however, was the eventual consequence of such late-night hedonism—you guessed it—having to lie down and hold my breath to zip up my Calvins.

This proved to be the direct inspiration for the creation of a magic muffin that could reverse the Ritz cracker–cream cheese spell. I don't know how Mom managed to deflate come summer, but the bran muffins that follow were my salvation. A month before the mid-June pagan celebration of *Vestalia*, festival of the first fruits, I would go on a *fruit-and-meltdown-muffin-and-cottage-cheese-and-oceans-of-water* sabbatical and pretend that I was doing it for some noble cause in honor of an obscure ancient goddess. In keeping with tradition (prayers are offered to Vesta before and after meals), I would toss in a prayer or two before eating my mood food, but in all honesty the petitions were more like, "Please help me get these crackers off my butt," and "Accept my sacrifice in the form of a little extra weight before bikini season." It worked.

This recipe looks a bit complex given the number of ingredients, but a crafty kitchen goddess can concoct it in less time than it takes to put on her bathing suit, go look in the mirror, and come back to the kitchen committed to getting those cells moving. And move they will; these meal-in-a-muffin hip-friendly goodies are the diet deity in my household.

Magic Meltdown Bran Muffins

⅓ cup whole wheat flour

⅔ cup unbleached white flour

1½ cups unprocessed oat or wheat bran

¼ cup wheat germ

¼ cup cornmeal

⅓ cup brown sugar

1 tablespoon baking powder

¾ teaspoon salt

¼ teaspoon ground cinnamon (optional)

2 eggs, beaten

2 tablespoons molasses

⅔ cup applesauce

1 tablespoon canola oil

1⅓ cups low-fat milk

½ cup carrots, finely grated

1 cup blueberries, fresh or frozen

½ cup cut-up fresh fruit—apricots, peaches, bananas, mangoes—whatever strokes your mood or you have in the house.

Preheat oven to 375°F. In a large mixing bowl, blend the flours, bran, wheat germ, cornmeal, brown sugar, baking powder, salt, and cinnamon, if using. In another large bowl, combine the eggs, molasses, applesauce, oil, and milk. Pour the wet into the dry and mix gently. Just when everything comes together, stop stirring. Blend in the carrots and fruit, and don't be overly zealous about mixing.

Scoop batter into greased or papered muffin tins, filling them to the top (this helps achieve grand, mushrooming muffin tops). Bake for 20 to 25 minutes, until a toothpick comes out clean or the muffin springs back when touched. To store, put muffins in a Ziploc plastic bag and keep frozen until desired. They are definitely tastier when warm; reheat in the microwave on HIGH for about 25 seconds.

Makes 1 dozen muffins.

A LA GODDESS

* Feel free to substitute ¼ cup honey for the brown sugar. If you do this, blend honey with other wet ingredients when mixing.

Mystic Transformation Meditation

Come embark upon a resistless rendezvous with yourself in a place that is glowing, perfected, cleansed, redeemed, shining with bliss—a place of grace; a place where all cravings are satiated, all problems resolved (know that the Latin root of resolve is *solvere*, which means release). Every day for six minutes, close your eyes, breathe, calm the mind chatter, enter into yourself—the temple of the soul—and whisper all or part of this powerful prayer as the powers of the earth and skies and universe listen.

Come, goddess, spirit of light
beloved of my soul,
I beseech you to
enlighten me, guide me, fill me with love,
whisper your will into my heart
fill my soul with vision.

Luxury is stillness and silence.

—Colette

Sister Love's
Travellin' Salvation Diet

*M*y friend Kim once wrote to me, "I wish the terms 'eating for emotional reasons' or 'emotional eating' had never developed into negative, 'bad for you' phrases. Cooking and eating should be an emotional expression of love and joy and accomplishment and feelings of thankfulness."

Let's say, goddess to goddess, that you are feeling a bit muddled physically, and you simply want to set the burden down; you are willing to let the excess physical weight—and the mental cargo that travels with owning extra pounds—melt away into a river of shining peace. Allow me a few loving suggestions:

* Behold the beauty of your body with the self-embracing spirit of generosity. May this book offer the invitation to eat and cook for balance and bliss. Food should never be a matter of deprivation, despair, or self-loathing, but rather an opportunity for nourishment and awareness.

* Treat yourself—pun definitely intended—to JoAnna Lund's book, *H.E.L.P.: Healthy Exchanges Lifetime Plan.* This humorous and sincere guide to the strategy planning necessary for releasing that which is no longer useful, offers valuable,

nifty tips on converting full-fat recipes to fighting-weight, feel-good foods. She has included a healthy dose of her own recipes for inspiration.

* Remember, the source of life—water—is your best kitchen aid; it is an instrument of purification, transformation, and refinement. Water has the magical property of flushing out toxins and the negativity harbored by them. So drink up, friends.

* Take the Kitchen Goddess Manifesto to heart. We need to fall back in love with our food, the cooking process, and ourselves. Allow the superabundance of the universe to find its way into your life. Consider the adage: Change your thoughts and you change your destiny.

* And, as Aunt June says, "Watch your portions, dear."

Communion, union with divinity,
is accomplished by means of food.
Taking food into the body is a ritual way of
absorbing the god into oneself.

—Thomas Moore, *Care of the Soul*

The wind greets me in a thunderous rush of being.

—My mantra since I was ten years old

The Beauty of the Blues

*T*his dinner possesses the ability to embrace feelings of loneliness and transform them into a nurturing state of aloneness, quietude, peace. Before preparing this lovely pasta dish, uncork a wonderful Chianti, Brunello, Barbaresco, or any other favorite red wine for yourself.

blueplatespecial

¼ pound pasta, capellini or spaghetti

Kosher salt

3 tablespoons olive oil

2 cloves garlic, minced

1 small onion, diced

Half a jalapeño pepper, diced (optional)

2 teaspoons double-concentrated tomato paste (available in tubes)

2 tablespoons raw pine nuts

Freshly ground pepper

1 to 2 tablespoons Parmigiano-Reggiano cheese, freshly grated

1 sprig fresh basil, chopped

Fill a large pot with water, cover and bring to boil. Add a pinch of kosher salt, allow the water to return to a boil, and add the pasta. Cook until al dente.

Simultaneously, heat the oil over medium heat in a large heavy saucepan. Add garlic and cook until golden brown, then add onion and the optional jalapeño and cook until onion is translucent. Stir in tomato paste and let simmer for about 10 minutes.

Toast the pine nuts in a small, hot, dry skillet until golden brown. Remove immediately and add to the simmering sauce so they can infuse it with their trademark flavor.

Drain the pasta and stir it into the olive oil sauce until all pasta is well coated. Season with 6 to 8 turns of a pepper mill and toss. Allow pasta to cook in the olive oil sauce for 4 to 5 more minutes. Adorn with grated cheese and freshly chopped basil; toss gently. Serve in a warmed bowl.

Makes 1 serving.

A Working Girl Has to Eat

Next time you're in the kitchen, pressed for time, and trying to think of a creative way to unclutter your pantry and toss together a quick pick-me-up dinner, why not whip up a plate of pasta putanesca with its robust sauce of olives, garlic, tomatoes, capers, and anchovies? When the pasta's done boiling, your sauce will be done.

Be advised, however, that this might not be the prim dish to order in a trendy Italian restaurant. Claiming its origins in the slums of Naples, *pasta putanesca* is proof that a busy working girl can even conjure up a meal between clients—it may be translated as Whore's Pasta.

And whatever you ask in prayer,
you will receive, if you have faith.

— Matthew 21:22

Shameless Culinary Comforts

*A*ffectionately known as Kim's Soul Slop in honor of the incorrigible kitchen goddess who flipped me the recipe, this is one of those divinely diabolic comfort dishes that escorts finesse and culinary correctness right out with yesterday's fad foods.

With all due respect, reduced-fat Bisquick baking mix isn't such a licentious aid to have hidden in the kitchen—it's simply an engineered blend of flour, soybean and cottonseed oil, leavening, salt, and dehydrated buttermilk. I add a pinch of saffron for integrity. Nevertheless, this shameless goddess remained proudly defiant when sharing her secrets, stating, "I've never done much by the book anyway."

Chipped Beef and Saffron Biscuits

Biscuits

I cup reduced-fat Bisquick baking mix

⅓ cup plus I tablespoon milk

½ teaspoon sugar

½ teaspoon saffron

I tablespoon butter, softened

Chipped Beef and Gravy

2 tablespoons butter

3 tablespoons flour

1½ cups milk

3 ounces sliced dried beef, cut or ripped into strips

Salt and pepper to taste

Preheat oven to 425°F. To make the biscuits, mix all ingredients together until a soft dough forms, adding a bit more baking mix if the dough is too sticky. On a surface dusted with baking mix, knead dough a few times and roll to a ½-inch thickness. Cut biscuits out with a round cookie cutter and place on an ungreased baking sheet. Bake for 7 to 10 minutes until biscuits are an appealing golden brown.

Makes 4 biscuits.

While biscuits are baking, make the beef and gravy. Melt the butter over low heat in a heavy skillet or saucepan. Blend in flour and continue stirring for 2 to 3 minutes. *Slowly* whisk in milk; bring to a simmer, whisking constantly. Add beef. Cook until sauce begins to thicken. Then, give it a dash of salt and freshly ground pepper and voila! It's slop time! Pull the shades and pour beef and gravy over hot biscuits.

Serves 1.

A LA GODDESS

* If you prefer not to ingest dried beef, try smoked turkey or proscuitto. Certainly you'll reach the same epicurean heights as do the unabashed beefivores lurking about (to whom I say, "The Armour dried beef that is packaged in a jar deserves an honorable mention"). The kitchen goddess Kim also proudly admits she often uses Lawry's seasoned salt in place of regular salt when she has it on hand.

The Sweet Taste of Daydreams

I am an armchair culinary traveler extraordinaire, using flavors of certain foods to transport me cerebrally to exotic lands and mythical places. I try to eat my way directly to Italy as often as possible, and do so enjoy the tequila sunrises of Zihuatanejo, Mexico. Whenever I am fortunate enough to get my sugar tongs on imported amber sugar crystals, I am having high tea in an English estate, and luxuriate on the Cote d'Azur with each creamy spoonful of a crème brûlée.

During mango season, you can find me under an umbrella palm, giant slow-motion leaves waving in a dripping hot, lazy, deep-tropics breeze. Irate monkeys scold me from the branches of a nearby mango tree for having just plucked a basketful of their prized, precious, fleshy fruits. The year, 1976; the place, a village called Tanjay on Negros Island in the Visayas of the Philippine archipelago. The mangos are the size of cantaloupes, and the juice is dripping down my neck, onto my body . . .

Suddenly, my dog is lapping the pudding-drenched spoon that has fallen to my side during my daydream. As the monkey chatter fades and the warm winds dissipate, I notice an impeccably licked empty bowl next to me. I guess she chased the monkeys away after she helped herself to a serving of Mango Tapioca Pudding I had on my lap.

Mango Tapioca Pudding

¼ cup quick-cooking tapioca

1¼ cups milk

1 egg, beaten

1 tablespoon honey or 5 teaspoons sugar

Half a large, ripe mango

1 tablespoon unsweetened applesauce

3 to 4 shakes ground cinnamon

A few drops pure vanilla extract (optional)

Pinch ground nutmeg

Whipped cream (optional)

Mix the tapioca, milk, honey, and egg in a heavy saucepan and set mixture aside while you dice the mango. Then bring the tapioca mixture to a full boil over medium heat, stirring constantly. Don't stop stirring—don't even answer the phone if it rings—to insure you do not burn the pudding.

Add the applesauce and cinnamon. Stir for a minute, remove from heat, and add the mango and vanilla, if using. Cool for at least 15 minutes (pudding thickens as it cools). Apportion tapioca into long-stemmed glasses or a decorative bowl and garnish with a sprinkle of nutmeg. Refrigerate or serve warm; top with whipped cream if you're feeling lavish.

Makes 1 lusty serving or 2 modest servings.

There cannot be a crisis next week;
my schedule is already full.

—Henry Kissinger

A magnum a day keeps the doctor away.

> —Baron Henry de Montesquieu
> of Möet & Chandon

The Immortal Pleasure of Bubbly
and Butter Cookies

*A*hhh . . . Champagne . . . the only alcohol Marilyn Monroe would touch . . . Empress Josephine's unabashed passion . . . "The only wine that leaves a woman beautiful after drinking it." Ahhh . . . Champagne . . . Madame Lily Bollinger—of Bollinger RD fame, of course—addressed this fruit of the vine most exquisitely when she explained, "I only drink Champagne when I'm happy and when I'm sad. Sometimes I drink it when I'm alone. When I have company, I consider it obligatory. I trifle with it if I'm not hungry and drink it when I am. Otherwise, I never touch it—unless I'm thirsty." Go girl! The origins, endless legends, and ritzy stories about this spirited, ritualistic sparkling wine render it even *more* potent and promising.

As do other legendary recipes that can be traced back to a time when gilt-edged goddesses frolicked through their days, shortbread—a very classy butter cookie—also possesses an alluring mystique. In the ancient days of pagan sun worship, this treat was a properly prepared sacrificial cake made of fine oatmeal with the notched edges symbolizing the rays of the sun. Imagine what spellwork was involved in creating authentic shortbread in Scotland centuries ago—no swank frivolity here—collecting the wood to fuel the ovens, choosing the stones upon which it was baked, churning the butter, and learning to discern the proper texture and color of flours and castor sugars.

Like a deck of Tarot cards, a shortbread mold—the essential tool in baking this Scottish hallmark—is reputed to be infused with more undiluted divinatory powers—will it help you bake a better cake?—when received as a gift. If you must purchase your own beautifully adorned ceramic pan with the delicate insignia and lacy imprints, superstition dictates that the magic of the mold be seasoned by baking three shortbreads and giving them all away before partaking of any biscuit made by your own hand.

No food brings out the luminary in me as Champagne and shortbread do when taken together. My tradition has always been to indulge in shortbread and champagne on the Celtic spring feast of Beltane, also known as May Day—the goddess celebration of fertility, rebirth, and the dance of life—and at random, inspired moments when the wild woman in me wants to come out and play.

Shortbread and Champagne

1 bottle of your favorite Champagne	½ teaspoon lemon extract (optional)
1 cup butter, softened	2½ cups unbleached white flour
½ cup sugar	1 tablespoon milk

Put your favorite Champagne on ice long before preheating the oven to 325°F. *By hand,* cream the butter and sugar with a large fork until light and fluffy. Add the lemon extract if desired. Delicately add the flour, and dribble in the milk. Knead the dough in your hands for a minute or two. The warmth of your hands will bring the dough to a beautiful consistency. This is the time to disperse your desires into the dough.

Press the dough into a lightly greased ceramic shortbread pan that has been sprinkled with sugar. Prick the surface with a fork and make your wish *du jour*.

Bake for 25 to 30 minutes until golden brown. Let cool for at least 10 minutes before loosening the edges with a knife. Gently invert the pan onto a plate. Cut the shortbread while still warm into serving pieces along the decorative imprints of the mold.

Makes 1 cake (most molds imprint 8 individual biscuits). Store shortbread in an airtight tin.

A la Goddess

* Activate the magic around you by lighting candles, opening a window, letting a water fountain flow (if you have one), and placing a favorite stone, crystal, or vase full of flowers on the table. On a table covered with linen and bathed in candlelight, adorn a most treasured plate with a wedge or two of shortbread.

  Open your Champagne, pour a glass, and toast yourself, your desires, your dreams. Sybaritically nibble on the shortbread while sealing your fantasies with sips of bubbly. Relish the moment and smile with your eyes.

* Splits of champagne provide a resourceful alternative to drinking a full bottle. Remember, to open a good bottle of Champagne, hold the bottle at a 45-degree angle (*"Like an erection,"* a saucy society matron once whispered to me at a fundraising gala with a politically incorrect gleam in her eye), and turn the bottle, not the cork. This will prevent precious overflow and the possibility of renegade corks flying about the room.

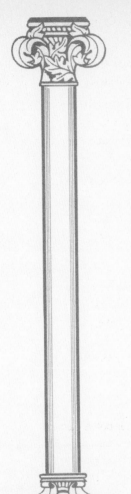

CHAPTER 6

The Artemis Party

FUN FARE
FOR
FESTIVE OCCASIONS

We are most governed when we are most wild.

—John Muir

Artemis of the brilliant moonlight, lady of all wild things, mistress of beasts, a lion unto women, protector of the meek, and goddess of the hunt requests the honor of your presence at her party. No shoes, pretenses, or make-up are required. Clothing is optional. Freedom is optimal. Bring your most spirited friends, your most open mind, and your best brand of humor.

Be prepared for divine dining with the three Graces present—Splendor, Mirth, and Good Cheer. Apollo will make heavenly music on his golden lyre, Hermes will serve a feast suited for all Olympians, and Aphrodite will tell us the real secret of why she was awarded the Golden Apple. Niké, the goddess of victory, might drop in accompanied by the nine Muses and that infamous hedonist, Pan. Water bowls and bones will even be set out for his band of hunting hounds. It will be a constellation of fun. No regrets.

If you were to throw a dream party—no stress allowed—who would you invite and what would you serve? Would it be a four-course extravaganza prepared and served with the help of wood nymphs; a chili, ponita, and corn bread football feast; or a felicitously random *ambigu*—a buffet meal at which various, often *unrelated*, dishes are served? Would you invite three people or ten? Which of your signature dishes and desserts would you lavish upon your merrymakers?

Just remember, the key ingredients for a party of this caliber are carefree good cheer, relaxed revelry, and insouciant surrender to the influence of the quintessential wild woman and goddess of the moon, Artemis. Come . . . the moon is rising.

A Melting Pot of Fun

My friend Melissa has been known to throw some of the best parties in the Lake Tahoe basin. Her trademark mix of people, conversations, music, refreshments, and food dances away with the prize every time; you *remember* her parties. They are better than getting a massage—relaxing, fortifying, never a place for pretension or worry.

The secret is simple: for every great party, there is a sensible, doting hostess or host who knows exactly how to enthrall the guests. It is paramount to entertain in an atmosphere that is comfortable yet a tad unusual, accented with fabulous feasts that are often thematic or ethnic (Miss is Norwegian) and *always* fun and festive. When Melissa whips up—or shall we say, melts down—the recipe for her sister's Swiss fondue for a center-stage appetizer, everyone *raves*.

I think the appetence for Swiss fondue involves an intricately conditioned taste, yet I believe that any wise kitchen goddess should learn to perfect a great fondue and set it out at parties in place of faddish appetizers. It complements both meatless and meat-filled main courses, it's easy, and it's still a unique fare. Fondue is a frolicsome, social art-form, deserving of culinary perfection.

Because Swiss fondue is traditionally a cooler-weather comfort, my custom is to refrain from serving it between May Day and the opening kick-off of football season. When the afternoon shadows grow longer, and the fall winds begin to rustle the leaves in the trees, I shine up the fondue pot, gather the fondue forks, and put away the barbie. Daylight savings time means Swiss fondue time to me. This is the recipe inspired by a fun-fest at Melissa's place.

Aleta's Swiss Fondue

Half a clove garlic, pressed

2 cups dry white wine

1¼ pounds Swiss cheese, cut into cubes

½ cup kirschwasser

3 tablespoons cornstarch

¼ teaspoon baking soda

White pepper to taste

Paprika to taste

Ground nutmeg

6 to 8 tart apples, sliced

2 loaves sourdough French bread,
  cut into 1½-inch cubes

A fondue pot with forks

Heat the garlic and the white wine in a saucepan over medium-low heat. Add the Swiss cheese to the wine, a handful of cubes at a time, stirring constantly as it melts. Mix the kirsch and cornstarch together; add to the fondue and bring to a low boil, stirring constantly. When all ingredients are blended, turn off heat, add baking soda, and stir. Season with a few shakes each of white pepper, paprika, and nutmeg.

Light the fondue pot fire, pour the melted cheese mixture into the pot, and let the party begin. Display the bread cubes and apple slices around the pot.

Serves 6.

Cooking is a way of giving—and making yourself desirable.

—Michel Bourdin

At my age, I enjoy every day.
When I'm really smart,
I enjoy every moment.

—Dorismarie Welcher, "Queen of the Hudson"

The Art of a Perfect Party

I don't want to sound like a *Rules* girl, but there are a few proven secrets that, if followed, have the power to dazzle even the crustiest crowd of culinary elitists at your next party.

Polish the ambience with great music, candles, and flowers everywhere—even in the bathroom. Fill the house with the aroma of fresh bread by popping one of those grocery-store thaw-and-bake loaves of bread into the oven. (Don't serve it, however, or you'll lose your goddess status immediately.)

Make a great impression with the first drink. Use dramatic glasses, such as foot-high Champagne flutes or an assortment of cut-glass flea-market treasures. Keep the selection of drinks and spirits simple—Champagne, dry martinis, mineral water mixed with homemade lemonade, vodka twists.

Go ethnic and/or always serve a family recipe. Most people don't possess the authentic taste capacity necessary to judge a particular ethnic dish, unless of course it is from their culture. No one will dare criticize your Grandmother's ham.

Serve an assortment of dynamite dinner rolls and breads—rye, sourdough, whole grain, pumpernickel, or buttermilk biscuits (the biscuits can be whipped up in no time).

Unless you are a bread wizard and have the time to bake it, I recommend buying bread from the best—European, if possible—bakery in town. Serve rolls and baguettes in a nice basket lined with linen.

Always pour two different types of red wine; people like to compare their wines. You can up the ante by making one of them foreign and one domestic.

Serve a very traditional dessert; again, something that Mom would have made—apple pie à la mode (with the best ice cream you can scoop) always works wonders.

Install a dimmer switch.

Rockin' with the Goddess

"Sugar Magnolia"	"Bread 'n' Butter"
"Strange Brew"	"Strawberry Fields Forever"
"Cinnamon Girl"	"No Sugar Tonight"
"American Pie"	"Pasta on the Mountain"
"Sweet Painted Lady"	"Spoonful"
"Cold Turkey"	"Honey Don't"
"Stir It Up"	"Sweet Melissa"
"Cleanup Time"	"Sweet Surrender"
"Sweet Jane"	"Cheeseburger in Paradise"
"Peaches en Regalia"	"Sticky Fingers"
"Sugar Pie Honey Bunch"	"You Can Tune a Piano but You Can't Tuna Fish"
"How Sweet It Is"	

Free Advice Is
Just That

*T*hough entirely capable of orchestrating a fabulous feast, Hera, queen consort of the Heavens, was usually too busy trying to keep her licentious and prolific husband under control. I've never understood, given her stature and supreme presence, why didn't she just "kick back and enjoy." In light of the fact, she was "motivated by a goddess-given instinct toward marriage" and saw her role as being the loyal "until death do us part" wife (and, as gods and goddesses are immortal, this meant *eternity*), the main ingredient in life—love—was elusive for Hera. But rule the universe she did; ambitiously, determinedly, and with a fiery eye that didn't miss much.

This all tickles my mind with thoughts of Martha Stewart. The woman has style; the woman is an inspiration to many. One alleged Martha groupie, Lynda Goldstein, an assistant professor of English and women's studies at Penn State University's Wilkes-Barre campus and co-author of *Reading Martha Stewart: It's a Good Thing,* has even likened her social prowess to that of Thomas Jefferson. But, I became a tad concerned when I read Lynda quoted as saying, "There's something grounded and admirable about her . . . But I'm not going to go out and do a Martha Stewart dinner. There are limits to my fandom." I was disappointed to hear that Martha scared her off.

I, a goddess in the kitchen, am undaunted by this domestic icon and would, in fact, welcome the opportunity to dazzle her with good cheer and great food. We are very different women, but this shouldn't deter us from sharing a few good laughs. I realized this the first time I watched her program and, glorious and pretty in her hip waders, she said,

"Now we're going to go out and pick cranberries from the cranberry bog for our cranberry bread." Hip waders? Cranberry bog? I'd rather wait here by the mixing bowl, if you don't mind.

Though I respect her in a detached way, her eventual flight from my fancy occurred while I was living in Tahoe, where unmerciful amounts of snow fall during the High Sierra winters. I had just spent two hours digging my car out from under the infamous "Sierra cement" and was back inside savoring a warm cup of tea when I read a "Martha-ism" in the newspaper: "Always leave an inch of snow so it looks nice and white. Esthetics are very important in snow removal." Thank you for the blizzard advice, but I ask you now, "Is this *really* such a *good thing?*"

With my hat off to her—and my shovelling task accomplished— here's my response to Martha's free advice. My kitchen goddess friend Kim, who whipped this one up, says people *always* ask her to make it and she swears there are *never* any leftovers . . . snow or no snow, chill the wine.

Killer Krab Salad

8 ounces crab meat	I tablespoon sugar
¾ cup sour cream	3 hard-boiled eggs, chopped
¾ cup Miracle Whip salad dressing	I cup celery, chopped
I small onion, finely chopped	Salt and pepper to taste

Mix all ingredients together and serve in a fun bowl accompanied by an assortment of crackers, a freshly baked baguette, and carrot and celery slices. Uncork a nicely chilled Pinot Grigio and let the wine flow like wine should. Enjoy! Serves 4.

A la Goddess

* Feel free to use imitation or real crab, low-fat or full-fat mayo, sugar or sugar substitute on this one (might depend on your audience). Substitute a packet of Sweet-n-Low or Equal for the sugar, if so desired—and, rest assured, imitation crab tastes perfectly delicious and is practically undetectable.

Heating Up the Joint

I eagerly waited in heated anticipation for years for Cayenne Pete, aka Quah-man, aka Peter Perkins, aka kitchen demigod, to give me his salsa recipe. Peter and I have one quality in common: We both like to dose ourselves with Tabasco until our eyeballs sweat. I don't dare suggest that you use the amount that Pete and I would normally use in this fire bath of vegetables and spices. Cayenne Pete says: "Mix the seasoning potion to taste—it takes practice. *Sense* what you are preparing; *feel* the mood of your dining audience; *be* all that is good in the food you prepare."

Be forewarned: when Peter picks his peck of peppers, he marinates them in Tabasco and throws them all in the salsa. Proceed with caution and make sure the bathtub is full of ice-cold beer or water . . . things can really heat up at Cayenne Pete's house.

Cayenne Pete's Original Salsa

2 pounds fresh ripe tomatoes, seeded
  and chopped

½ pound tomatillos, seeded and chopped

1 large white onion, chopped

1 red bell pepper, chopped

½ cup chopped scallions

The Seasoning Potion

2 jalapeño peppers, 1 green, 1 red,
  seeded and minced

1 bunch fresh cilantro, stems removed
  chopped

2 to 3 cloves garlic, minced

1 teaspoon ground cumin

Tabasco sauce

Combine the tomatoes, tomatillos, onion, bell pepper and scallions in a large bowl. Mix the spice potion to taste and add to the salsa. Chill and enjoy! Feel free to add more of this or less of that in order to keep the peace with the taste buds. Serve with your favorite chips in a large, decorative bowl.

Serves 4 to 6 (makes approximately 2 cups salsa)

One of the best antidotes . . . is to
decide the person you like best to drink with
and . . . have a pre-dinner nip with her or him, alone . . .
sit back and absorb a little quick relaxation from a glass
and then eat, quaffing immortality and joy.

—M. F. K. Fisher

A Fun Football Feast

*I*f you are planning a famed football feast, ponitas are an integral ingredient to the fun. First of all, you can host a contest to see how fast your guests can assemble ten of them. This helps keep the pre-game jitters to a buzzing minimum. Second, they're *blindfold fare*—easy, easy, easy. Third, and most notably, the taste of ponitas simply makes love to salsa and an ice-cold beer.

Ponitas

2 cups (8 ounces) sharp cheddar cheese, grated

1½ cups mayonnaise

1 cup green onions, chopped

4 to 5 shakes Old Bay seasoning

2 French baguettes or loaves of sourdough bread, cut into ½-inch slices

Paprika to taste

Preheat the oven to 400°F. In a large bowl, mix the cheese, mayonnaise, onions, and Old Bay seasoning together. Spread on the bread and garnish with paprika. Place the bread slices on a large, flat baking sheet and bake for approximately 10 minutes, until instinct tells you they are ready to eat. Serve warm. Depending on the length of the baguettes, makes 18 to 24 ponitas.

A la Goddess

* Reduced-fat ingredients are fine if the diet devil is hanging on your shoulder. But we all know the real thing is the best. As Donna the Ponita doyenne says, "Don't substitute. It only 'costs' a little more to go first class."

**The first rule of winning:
Don't beat yourself.**

—Football adage

Eat, friends, drink, and
be drunk with love.

—Song of Solomon 5:1

Still Life with Chili

$\mathcal{Y}$ears ago, when I lived in Aspen, my roadbuddy Dorismarie and I would entertain ourselves by jumping in the car to escape "Glitter Gulch" and drive around western Colorado in search of the perfect bowl of chili. She had one very definite prerequisite standard for her chili—it could not move in the bowl. Being in a part of Colorado that many Mexican Americans called home, we often practiced our gourmandise at Mexican restaurants. Speaking no Spanish except the word "chili"—oh, yes, and "dos mas Margaritas por favor!"—we'd put in our order and look forward to our big bowls of thick, spicy, chunky, hearty chili.

Let it be known, if you want chili that doesn't move, the kind we think of when we say "chili," don't search for it at a Mexican restaurant. If you see "pork green or red chili" on the menu, be assured that this runny, tomato-based stew is not what you're looking for. Like Dorothy returning home from Oz, we finally realized that, given the number of Texas natives in Aspen, the best chili to be found in Colorado was in our own backyard on Ajax Mountain at an elevation of ten thousand feet.

So, the next time you're feeling footloose and fancy-free and just want to spice up your life a tad, pack up and head straight for one of the many chili cook-off contests, the Lone Star State, Aspen, or your kitchen with this recipe. This dandy improvisation on the recipe from Bonnie's Restaurant on Aspen Mountain definitely fulfills our vision of the perfect bowl of chili.

Fancy-Free Aspen Chili

2 pounds ground chuck or turkey, or 4 chicken breasts (bone and skin removed), chopped

2 tablespoons olive oil

¼ cup brown sugar

1½ teaspoons ground cinnamon

1 large onion, chopped

2 stalks celery, chopped

1 green pepper, chopped

1 yellow or red pepper, chopped

1 can (4 ounces) diced green chilies

1 tablespoon garlic powder

1 tablespoon chili powder

2 teaspoons ground cumin

2 teaspoons dried oregano leaves

1½ teaspoons salt

1 teaspoon white pepper

2 bay leaves

2 cans (28 ounces each) tomatoes, chopped but not drained

1 can (16 ounces) tomato sauce

1 can or bottle of beer

¼ teaspoon baking soda

1 pound white kidney or Great Northern beans, soaked overnight and drained— about 4 cups total—or 2 cans (15 ounces each) of your favorite beans

Tabasco sauce, salt, and spices à la desire

Chopped onions, grated cheese, and sour cream for garnish (optional)

In a large, seasoned caldron, heat the oil and brown the meat, sprinkling on the sugar and cinnamon while the meat is cooking. Add the onion, celery, peppers, canned chilies, remaining spices, and bay leaves, and simmer over low heat for about 15 minutes, until everything starts smelling and looking good. Add tomatoes, tomato sauce, and beer and cook for a few minutes. Add baking soda and stir well; the chili will bubble and boil as if it's alive. When it's done acting up, add the soaked beans (if you are using canned beans, do *not* add them yet!) Simmer uncovered for approximately 2 hours or until beans are thoroughly cooked.

If you are using canned beans, drain and add them after the chili has cooked for about 1½ hours. Remove bay leaves. Feel free to exercise your alchemical savvy by adding more spices. Serve with favorite garnishes—onions, grated cheese, sour cream—and accompany with corn bread, ice cold beer in frosty mugs or glasses, or, of course, Margaritas.

Serves 6 to 8.

I must divide Perfect Dinners into three categories . . .
gastronomical perfection can be reached in these combinations:
one person dining alone, usually upon a couch or a hillside;
two people, of no matter what sex or age, dining in a good restaurant;
six people, of no matter what sex or age, dining in a good home.

—M. F. K. Fisher, *The Art of Eating*

It's kind of fun to do the impossible.

—Walt Disney

The Wild Blue Bread

*W*hen shopping from food catalogues or in specialty stores, keep your eyes wide open in hopes of spotting blue cornmeal for baking this soulful staple. The uncommon color adds such a delicious twist to this sweet, flaky pan bread. If you find it, buy twice as much as you think you should—it makes a fun gift for friends. Then, head for the kitchen and bake lots of blue corn bread for the party!

Sweet Southern Corn Bread

1½ cups cornmeal or blue cornmeal	2 eggs
1 cup unbleached white flour	1 cup sour cream
¼ cup brown sugar	½ cup milk
1 teaspoon salt	¼ cup margarine or butter, melted
½ teaspoon baking soda	⅔ cup creamed corn
1 tablespoon baking powder	

Preheat oven to 400°F. In a large bowl and by hand, combine the dry ingredients and blend well. In a separate bowl, whisk the eggs, sour cream, and milk together.

Pour this mixture into the dry mix and stir languidly. Dribble the melted margarine into the bowl. Mix slightly before folding in the creamed corn. Pour the batter into a 9-inch, greased, cast-iron skillet. Bake for approximately 20 minutes or until a toothpick comes out clean.

Serves 6 to 8.

A la Goddess

* When I bake this on a creative whim, I often find myself without sour cream, so I concoct it by adding two tablespoons of vinegar or lemon juice to a cup of milk, and letting it rest for 10 minutes. As a substitute for the creamed corn, try fresh, cooked corn sliced from the cob, or cooked mashed squash or sweet potatoes!

* Authentic southern corn bread was usually made in an iron skillet on *top* of the stove. With an electric stove, this is a tricky task; with a gas stove I've had several successes cooking over low, low heat. Try it and let me know what you discover!

Kitchen Goddess Cooking Club

If the truth be known, I have never prepared a complete, beginning to end, recipe from a cookbook. All my recipes have been inspired, invented, borrowed, or given to me. Don't misread me—cookbooks are wonderful—but I am one for whom the hands-on method was invented. Food is imbued with a particular soul and for me to know it, I have to feel it. The best possible way to feel that spirit is for someone to share a recipe, and with it the secrets of making it, and then to enjoy the experience of eating it together.

It is around this idea that the original Kitchen Goddess Cooking Club was molded. Once a month, generally near the time of the full moon, our group of between three and six kitchen goddesses comes together with recipes and a special potluck favorite food in hand; each person has prepared either an appetizer, a refreshment, an entrée, or a dessert, and has copies of the recipe to share with the others.

The entrée assignment rotates from gathering to gathering; depending on schedules and interest, we either do the "lunch bunch" or meet for a nice dinner. The club gives us all the opportunity to help each other explore and create while indulging in great food, lively stories, and spirited fun surrounded by the supporting laughter of friends. I invite you to try it . . . and please share some of your cooking secrets and recipes with me.

No One Goes Home
Without a Smile

I love it when men come into the kitchen and play—the energy changes and leaps about. I lured this recipe away from my brother, who calls it Chicken à la Patricio, a signature dish of one of his friends. I've made some changes and rechristened it Chicken Olympus. It's the perfect dish for a man to prepare for Artemis' band of wild women.

In our classical version of Chicken Olympus, Hermes would be stirring the pot. I fancy this mischievous god, in his winged sandals with golden Caduceus-mixing spoon in hand, nude and beardless, cooking up a storm. Because it was believed that he possessed magical powers over sleep and dreams and was a tried-and-true trickster—he had a fine knack for transforming himself into a sacrificial goat in hopes of tumbling the Greek princess Driope—we'd have to keep our eyes on him to insure he didn't slip something extra into the pot.

We could also count on Hermes to be a good conversationalist, given the fact that he was the Greek god of oratory. Add to this that he was responsible for good luck and wealth, and was—along with his brother Apollo, another cutie—the patron god of athletes, we know he'd work the party with a gentle ease. He, Artemis, and Pan, Apollo's rollicking half-animal offspring that all the gods adored, would have a merry time. The rest of the guests would bask in the delight of a dish well done.

Chicken Olympus

8 chicken breasts, bone and skin removed

1 can (28 ounces) crushed tomatoes

½ pound fresh mushrooms, sliced

1 cup cream, half-and-half, or milk

1 tablespoon dried oregano

1 teaspoon curry powder

¼ teaspoon white pepper

1 box (10 ounces) frozen peas

Heat oven to 350°F. Slice breasts into bite-size tenders, and bake them in a covered dish for approximately 10 to 15 minutes, just until the meat turns white (take care not to overcook). Remove from oven.

In a large pot over medium-high heat, mix tomatoes, mushrooms, cream or milk, spices, and chicken; heat to a slow boil. Add frozen peas. Cook for a few minutes longer. Great over orzo or rice.

Serves 8.

How to arrange a Succulent Wild Woman evening: . . .
make your invitation succulent . . . meet us for an evening
of delicious food, abundant laughter, poetry, and inspiration . . .
food: chocolate, fruit, homemade bread, cheese.

—Sark, *Succulent Wild Woman*

The Soup Kitchen Gourmet

We all called Tim O'Neill the Soup Kitchen Gourmet. His place was known as Roy's Soup Kitchen because there was always something on the stove—or barbecue—and the door was always open to anyone with an appetite. The barbecue ribs were worth postponing plans for, the array of soups—turkey and split pea were my favorite—took the edge off any tough day, and the refrigerator was always full of Molson Export Ale. Hungry, wayward friends seemed to be able to smell the dinner telepathically and would converge after work, after play, after waking up, to fill their plates and time and enjoy some of the finest—and freest—food in town. The soup kitchen god ruled his realm; the sauce was on.

Of all the daily special headliners served at the soup kitchen, his top-secret, family spaghetti-and-meatball sauce was the specialty of the house. He would spend days working on one batch of his cousin Sharon's trademark sauce, properly anointing it with the vigilant attention any great creation should receive. The feast was served with vermicelli, garlic bread, a sturdy salad, and a free flow of beverages. In a gesture similar to the New Orleans practice called *lagniappe*—giving a small gift to a visitor in a jinx-clearing concession to keep unwelcome spells at bay—he would customarily pack up a jar of sauce-to-go for me, seeing to it that there were at least three meatballs in it.

Though I've taken the liberty of digressing from the original handwritten recipe scribed in the soup kitchen gourmet's own hand (I added more cheese, the acid-kicking soda, and the wine), the integrity of his family's top secret sauce remains intact. Whether or not I will be given clemency for stealing the recipe will be decided by the Fates.

Upstate Secret Sauce with Meatballs

Sauce

¼ cup olive oil

3 cloves garlic, minced

3 pork chops or 1½ pounds Italian
    sausage

2 cans (28 ounces each) whole
    tomatoes, crushed

2 cans (12 ounces each) tomato paste

2 cups water

2 tablespoons fresh chopped parsley

2 tablespoons brown sugar

¼ teaspoon dried, finely ground oregano
    (or more, but be careful)

Pinch of dried sweet basil

¼ teaspoon baking soda

½ to ¾ cup Parmesan cheese,

More water or a splash red wine,
    if desired

Meatballs

2 pounds ground beef

1 cup Italian-seasoned bread crumbs

3 eggs, beaten

2 to 3 cloves garlic, minced

¼ cup fresh parsley, finely chopped

¼ teaspoon dried, ground oregano

¼ teaspoon dried sweet basil

½ cup Parmesan cheese, grated
    (more if you want)

½ cup water

Salt and pepper to taste

In a large heavy pot, heat the oil, add the garlic, and brown the pork chops or sausage. Purée the tomatoes in a blender, or add them to the pot and crush them finely with a potato masher or the like. Stir in tomato paste. Add the 2 cups water, parsley, sugar, oregano, and basil. Simmer on low heat, covered, for 30 minutes or so.

Remove the pork chops or sausage, chop the meat, and return it to the pot. Add baking soda and stir sauce until it stops bubbling. (The soda reduces acidity and, thus, the likelihood of heartburn!)

While the sauce is cooking, make the meatballs. Mix all ingredients together and form golf ball-sized meatballs (larger is fine). Stir cheese into the sauce, add meatballs, cover, and simmer for at least an hour or until meatballs are cooked. Do not stir meatballs until they have cooked a bit. Add more water if you feel the sauce is becoming too thick. Or, if you happen to be enjoying a glass of red wine while you cook, pour in a splash.

Serves 4 to 6 with a lagniappe jar left over to give to a friend.

I count myself in nothing else so happy
As in a soul remembering my good friends.

—Shakespeare

A Wild, Wonderful Moon Party

*T*he Greeks and other earth-based cultures were wise enough to measure their lives by the cycles of the moon. Many moons ago, before witch hunts, church dogma, and the industrialization of life in general, women commonly held the power of the moon close to their spirits and bodies, calling on the goddesses of this luminous beacon to aid them—Artemis and Selene to bestow the power of the full moon, Persephone of the crescent moon, and the bewitching Hecate, grand goddess of the darkest night, to tell of the mysteries of the hidden lunar soul.

Today, we are at least aware that the moon's cycle is 28½ days, as is a woman's natural cycle (no, my goddesses, this is not *coincidence*). Lore holds that bread rises more consistently during the waxing moon. Indeed, life in general seems to *rise* better during the waxing moon; this is a time for creating and attracting. For when this beacon begins to wane—the period from the full moon to when the nights are devoid of that pale, silver light dancing across the sky—our appetite for life sometimes changes, too. We enter a zone of regeneration and a time for completion and release.

Once a month, when the moon is newest and the universe is listening and receptive to petition, my most spirited friends and I come together for a New Moon Goddess Celebration. Here we recharge, rededicate our intentions, and, often, pick up our cosmic e-mail messages (or as author Julie Cameron says, get our "marching orders"). The finest wine and Champagne flows, the sweetest treats abound, the rooms—or outside decks— are flooded with candlelight, and we share our secrets and desires, unjudged, in an atmosphere of trustful, gentle counsel. When inspired—the parties are always on a free-flow modality—we turn on the music, dance, and move our energy. At New Moon Goddess Celebrations, "goddess" is a verb: we *goddess*.

I urge everyone to create a time to gather with trusted friends and celebrate the fact that we can always start the moment anew, starting, finishing, attracting, releasing, loving, b-e-i-n-g, laughing. We can jump-start a project, leap from the highest plateau of any diet, decide to attract or dismiss a paramour, change our goals, and even learn how to prepare new recipes. For those of you who are frisky, playful, powerful, and open-hearted, I share two of the fastest-acting recipes for bliss I know: the New Moon Meditation and New Moon Cookies.

The New Moon Meditation can be shared among friends at a New Moon Goddess Celebration or be written privately in your journal when the moon is new, a time to inspirit new goals, ideas, and direction:

What do you want to release from your life?

What are you thankful for?

What do you wish to manifest?

New Moon Cookies

1 cup butter at room temperature

5 tablespoons sugar

2 teaspoons pure vanilla extract

2 tablespoons milk

½ teaspoon salt

2 cups unbleached white flour

2 cups pecans, finely chopped or ground

Powdered sugar

Preheat oven to 325°F. (350°F if you live in the mountains). Cream the butter, sugar, vanilla, milk, and salt together in a large bowl. Mix in flour and stir; then mix in pecans. Shape the dough into 1-inch crescents or roll into little balls of dough (I reserve the ball-shape for Full Moon parties). Bake on a parchment-lined cookie sheet for 20 minutes. Roll the cookies in a bowl of powdered sugar when hot, hot, hot out of the oven.

Makes about 2 dozen.

Cheerful looks make every dish a feast.

—Phillip Massinger

A Toast to Oprah

*I*t's a provocative question: If you could invite anyone to dinner to partake of a favorite food, who would you invite and what would you serve? Ask yourself and write to me; I'd *love* to know. I read once that the kitchen goddess Mollie Katzen said she would invite several famous chefs and food writers. I forget what she said she would serve, but if her thinking cap was on and working, she'd simply have asked them to bring potluck dishes. A friend said she would invite Tom Cruise, and serve him crème brûlée with chopsticks because it would take him forever to eat it (and I suppose she could feast her eyes all the while). I would invite Tina Turner for a dessert tête-à-tête with foot-high flutes of fine Champagne and platters full of chocolate rum truffles and strawberries. My inspired friend Liz envisioned Oprah at her table, and wanted to surprise her with a feel-good favorite that had never been served before in the history of forks and knives. So we set out to create a new dish as an offering to this fascinating female.

From this adventure, a delightful tradition evolved: For special occasions I now invent a culinary novelty and present the namesake recipe as a gift. It takes a few ounces of whimsy and wit spiced with a spoonful of research, mixed and marinated with a generous dollop of imagination—Einstein's favorite ingredient—and the discovery is so fun and rewarding!

Root Beer Roast Tenderloin

1 quart (32 ounces) root beer, the best you can find

1 cup chopped onions

Olive oil

2 pork tenderloins (1 to 1¼ pounds each)

2 teaspoons Dijon-style mustard

2 tablespoons vinegar

2 tablespoons unbleached white flour

6 bell peppers, 2 each green, red, and yellow, sliced

Garlic powder

Salt

In a large heavy saucepan, bring the root beer to a boil. After 10 minutes, add the onions and continue boiling the root beer, encouraging reduction. While this is going on, move the oven rack to the highest point in oven and preheat the oven at Broil.

Anoint a roasting pan with olive oil, place tenderloins in it, and sear them against the high heat for a few minutes on each side. Reduce heat to 300°F. Cover the pan with tin foil and move it to the center of the oven. Roast for 45 minutes.

As the meat is cooking, add the mustard and vinegar to the root beer sauce. Cook for 5 minutes. Baste the tenderloins with half of the root beer concoction, cover with foil, and return to oven, basting occasionally.

Remove ½ cup of the sauce from the pan on the stove top and add 1 tablespoon of the flour, mixing wildly to form a roux. Reduce the stove-top heat to medium and pour the roux back into the root beer sauce, whisking to prevent lumps. Continue simmering until the sauce thickens.

When there are about 20 minutes left, pour the thickened sauce onto the loins and finish cooking. Arrange the sliced bell peppers on a baking sheet, sprinkle with olive oil, garlic powder, and salt, and place in the oven.

When the pork is done, place it on a grand serving tray, and slice into 1¼-inch thick medallions. Cover with foil and set aside. Turn up the oven temperature and broil the peppers for 3 to 5 minutes at the top of the oven until they are slightly charred.

Place the roasting pan on the stove over medium-low heat. To make gravy, remove ½ cup of the sauce from the pan, add the remaining tablespoon flour, and again mix wildly to form a roux. Pour the roux into the roasting pan, whisking to prevent lumps. Pour into a decorative gravy boat and serve with the Root Beer Roast Tenderloin garnished by the rainbow of roasted bell peppers. A Santé, Oprah!

Serves 6.

A LA GODDESS

* On this note, you are honorably invited to a beautiful meal of Root Beer Roast Tenderloin served with roasted bell peppers of every persuasion, a lively coleslaw with mandarin oranges tossed in raspberry vinaigrette, sumptuous, hot, homemade buttermilk biscuits, and a crisp, cool tossed green salad of Romaine, tomatoes, and baby greens. The evening's finale will include Ben and Jerry's Purple Passion Fruit Sorbet crowned with wedges of warm, homemade shortbread topped with lots of laughter. From goddess to goddess, we toast to our happiness!

The invention of a new dish adds
more to the happiness of mankind
than the discovery of a star.

—Brillat-Savarin

A Delectably Dis-Spelling Dish

The exotic combination of taste, sensation, aroma, and texture of this amazingly uncomplicated concoction renders it a pleasure for the imagination as well as the palate. Preparing and partaking of this savory, funky dish transports me to the dark-night bayous outside New Orleans, where, if you are unfortunate enough to take a wrong turn, Hecate, "she who has power far off" and goddess of the crossroads, may lead you into a hoodoo night. This eerie image always makes me grateful to come back to the reality of the stove and the guests I'll be eating with.

A kitchen goddess, when confronted with the powers of the unknown, knows that garlic wards off ill-behaved spirits, kosher salt holds them at bay, and ginger tames the butterflies in an excitable stomach. Sweet potatoes get the blood flowing again, often erotically, and coconut has the power to give the spirits a taste of their own scare tactics. Have you ever looked into the spooky little "face" of a coconut? The name of this diabolical fruit is derived from *coco*, the Portuguese word for goblin. With all these ingredients in your arsenal, you will, at the very least, eat in peace.

Curry Sweet Potatoes with Chicken-Apple Sausage

1¾ cups water

1 to 2 jalapeño peppers, seeds and ribs removed, minced

1 clove garlic, minced

1 small onion, chopped

1 tablespoon fresh ginger, peeled and finely grated

1½ teaspoons curry powder (preferably Madras)

1 teaspoon kosher salt

1½ pounds sweet potatoes, peeled and diced

½ cup tender celery stalks, chopped

1 red or green pepper, chopped

¼ cup unsweetened coconut milk

1 pound chicken-apple sausage

1 pound asparagus or fresh green beans

Lime wedges

In a large saucepan, combine water, jalapeños, garlic, onion, ginger, curry powder, and salt. Bring to a boil. Add sweet potatoes, celery, and pepper, and simmer, covered, until potatoes are tender (about 15 minutes). Uncover and cook for about 5 minutes longer, allowing sauce to thicken. Add coconut milk and cook at barely a simmer for about 5 minutes.

Meanwhile, either boil the sausage until done or slice and fry until crisp. Steam asparagus or beans until tender. Arrange the vegetable and sausage on a plate and spoon the sweet potatoes and sauce over them. Garnish with lime wedges.

Serves 4.

A LA GODDESS

* Do all your chopping and measuring before the sun sets. After nightfall, fill the kitchen and dining room with candlelight.

A Wood Nymph's Delight

*T*he seemingly immortal, incidental divinities and nature spirits in the mythical smorgasbord, distinguished according to the elements they personified, were titled nymphs. Represented as young and beautiful maidens fond of gaiety, music, and dancing, they inhabited forests and fountains, the sea and streams, meadows and groves. These nature goddesses were often found in the company of the rural deities, namely Artemis, Apollo, Pan, Hermes, and of course, party-boy himself, Dionysus. Though they could impart inspiration and felicity on a good day, these frivolous fairies were perfectly capable of *Schadenfreude*—wicked glee in stirring up confusion in the hearts and minds of assorted boy toys. The dryads (tree nymphs) were particularly favored by Artemis, and would flit in the moonlight with her and her hounds.

A playful choice of dessert for all the sweet-toothed deities at a gathering has always been the Party Plant. The art of cultivating this potted dessert lies in choosing the finest flora, the pot, and the proper occasion to present it. When planted with an

imaginative eye, this ultimate April Fool's Day party dessert can surprise even the staunchest gardener and it is certain to appease the more affable appetites of forest nymphs and their consorts.

Party Plant

1 package (20 ounces) Oreo-type cookies

8 ounces cream cheese, at room temperature

¼ cup butter, softened

1 cup powdered sugar

2 packages (3.4 ounces each) instant vanilla pudding mix

3¼ cups milk

12 ounces Cool Whip-type topping

1 large plastic flower pot with no holes in the bottom

Real, plastic, or silk flowers

Crush the cookies in a blender (3 or 4 at a time) and dump the crumbs into a large bowl. In a separate bowl, combine the cream cheese, butter, and powdered sugar.

In yet another bowl, mix the instant vanilla pudding mix and milk together and let stand for 5 minutes. Mix in the Cool Whip. Fold the cream cheese mixture and the pudding mixture together gently.

Starting with the cookies at the bottom, begin the gardening process of filling your pot with alternate layers of "dirt" (cookies) and "mulch" (custard). Be sure to end with "dirt" on top.

Cover and place in the freezer for at least 2 hours before serving. Allow to "thaw" at least 20 minutes before serving, at which time you would garnish with your most beautiful bouquet! Dish with glee after using for decoration during dinner! Note: If you are traveling with your plant, I highly recommend that you do your gardening the night before the party and freeze the dirt overnight.

Serves 6 to 8.

Let the dishes be few in number, but exquisitely chosen.

—Brillat-Savarin

Saving the Best 'til Last

This banana cream pie inhabits the land of "the best ever," where other revered archetypal contestants, nestled in tantalizing intrigue, reside: the elusive, perfect, piquant lemon meringue (Ann Landers claims to possess the world's best, a recipe given to her by a New York cabbie), the "best-ever chocolate chip cookies" (we know we have that recipe right here in this book!), and the stimulating, top-shelf Margarita (Greg, the bar god at a local restaurant, can stir a flawless version of this potion).

Many years ago in the heart of Marin County in Northern California, I was served an ambrosial slice of that quintessential delicacy, the "best-ever" Banana Cream Pie. After dessert, when no one was keeping tabs on my antics, I pocketed the recipe and carried it off into the night.

Best-Ever Banana Cream Pie

One 9-inch pie crust (see page 104 for recipe)

3 cups whole milk

⅔ cup sugar

4 egg yolks

¼ cup cornstarch

1 package (8 ounces) cream cheese

1 teaspoon pure vanilla extract

2 teaspoons dark rum

Pinch of nutmeg

3 medium bananas, ripe yet firm

Juice of half a lemon (optional)

1 cup whipping cream

1 teaspoon sugar

Bake the pie crust at 400°F. for 7 to 9 minutes, cool and set it aside.

Combine the milk, sugar, egg yolks, and cornstarch in a heavy saucepan and whisk madly until mixture is frothy. Cook, stirring constantly, over low heat until mixture begins to boil and thickens enough to coat a metal spoon lightly. Add cream cheese and stir until melted, about 2 minutes. Remove from heat and add vanilla, rum, and nutmeg. Let cool to room temperature.

Slice the bananas and arrange them on the bottom of the baked pie shell. Sprinkle a wee bit of lemon juice over the bananas if you feel the urge. Pour the cooled custard over the bananas and chill for at least 2 hours.

Just before serving, whip the cream and sugar together until stiff, and garnish the pie with whipped cream. For the full ambrosial effect and taste of this pie, try eating a piece while blindfolded!

Serves 8.

A la Goddess

* The archetypal banana cream pie I tasted that night was garnished with 1 cup toasted shredded coconut rather than with whipped cream. Trust your choices.

* When baking the pie crust, prick bottom of pie several times with a fork. Place baking parchment over the dough and line with weights, uncooked rice, beans, or macaroni. Bake 7 minutes, remove weighting material and paper and bake 2 more minutes, until golden.

Blessed are the funky wild women,
for they make God laugh in delight;
Blessed are women of passion
for they teach others to hear God laugh in delight.

—Kimberly Terrell

CHAPTER 7

Charmed Holidays

CELEBRATIONS FOR A SPELL

Superstition is the poetry of life.

—Goethe

Nowhere is ritual more prevalent than in the recipes of holiday fare. Imagining a birthday without a cake, a Thanksgiving without a big, shared meal complete with assorted pies, or a Valentine's Day without chocolate leaves more than just an empty craving in the tummy; the soul is also left with a longing for sustenance.

The celebration of life's milestones would seem hollow without our cherished, traditional dishes. At what age is a baby conditioned to want cookies at Christmas, and from where do many of these extraordinary food traditions appear? I am still exploring the presence of oyster stew at our Christmas Eve table; logically, I know that it's a "family thing," but why the ritual of slurping fleshy, viscous mollusks drowning in a creamy pool of soup in anticipation of Christ's birthday? Since it's but once a year, I've managed to let my soup spoon rise all the way to the occasion of my reluctant lips—and *because it is tradition*, it all settles gently—eventually.

For a kitchen goddess, holiday cooking is a charmed event. Devoid of most of the obligatory pressures of day-to-day food preparation, this is an open-season for relaxed, joyous, and inspired creativity. When surrounded by friends and immersed in the energy of spirited fun, hope, and goodwill, we make holiday cooking intoxicating.

We start off our holiday cheer with Eighteen-Karat Egg Nog, a golden brew that is the smoothest, most potent, most festive drink I have ever poured; folks will talk about it for *years* after they taste it! It has served as a holiday ritual for years at the home of a friend, Jo Grieve, who shared the original recipe with me. On New Year's Eve, after I toast with Champagne, Eighteen-Karat Egg Nog is the next refreshment to make an appearance. To good luck and great friends!

Eighteen-Karat Egg Nog

9 large egg yolks

2½ cups superfine sugar

3⅓ cups (1 750 ml. bottle) Early Times bourbon

1½ cups plus 2 tablespoons (13 ounces) light rum

1½ cups plus 2 tablespoons (13 ounces) brandy

4 cups whipping cream

2 cups half-and-half

Freshly grated nutmeg

Whisk the yolks and the sugar together by hand in a large bowl (a 13-quart one works best). Slowly stir in the bourbon, rum, brandy, cream, and half-and-half. Ladle out a bit for inspiration. Pour the precious potion into glass jars and refrigerate, covered, for *at least* three days.

Shake it all up *very well* before serving. Serve over ice with a sprinkle of freshly grated nutmeg. Sip slowly and enjoy!

Makes 1 gallon (serves 12).

A la Goddess

*Only you can decide if drinking this glorious egg nog is worth the risk of salmonella poisoning associated with raw eggs. However, keep in mind that the high alcohol content of this potion greatly reduces the possibility of the presence of bacteria, and hence, the risk.

* I've had good results replacing superfine sugar with granulated sugar on occasion; I simply stir the egg yolks, sugar, and alcohols longer to allow the sugar to dissolve. Feel free to use less sugar (2 to 2¼ cups) if you so desire. The egg nog will still pack a happy punch!

* Keep in mind, the longer it ages, the better it tastes. The egg nog will keep, refrigerated, for up to a year. Cheers!

Cooking is . . . sculpture of the soul.
A good cook works by the fire of the imagination,
not merely by the . . . fire in the stove.

—Robert Tristram Coffin, *Mainstays of Maine*

The Original Chicken Stew for the Soul

*T*his old Pennsylvania Dutch secret family classic, which my nana lackadaisically called "Chick'n Pop-Eye," simply spells "home." It provides a grounding touchstone every time it's served. Eating this always zips me back to the happiest moments of my childhood—home and warm, weaving plans on a chilly Sunday afternoon after I had been riding my pony Goldie all morning.

Though handy for filling the bellies of a large, hungry family, this stew serves as a perfect traditional cockles-warmer on New Year's Day when visitors happen by for well-wishing or to watch college football games. Add some homemade Olympic Squaw Bread or Sweet Potato Bread, and pour the Eighteen-Karat Egg Nog or Fire Sign Wine, and "touchdown!" Happy, happy New Year.

Chick'n Pop-Eye

1 chicken or 4 chicken breasts	1 teaspoon salt
2½ to 3 quarts water	Dash of mace
2 chicken bouillon cubes	1 tablespoon cold butter
½ onion, chopped	2 eggs
4 cups unbleached white flour	1 cup milk

In a large pot, cover the chicken with water, and bring to a full boil. Reduce heat, add chicken bouillon cubes and onion, and continue cooking chicken at a low boil until chicken is done, but not quite "fallin' off the bones," approximately 30 minutes. Turn off the heat; remove the chicken from broth and remove skin and bones. Cut up and return to the broth—heat still off.

Mix flour, salt, and mace in a large bowl. Crumble the butter into the flour with a fork, and add the eggs and milk. Mix with a *strong* wooden spoon until the dough is smooth. Divide dough into four portions to make it easy to work with. On a well-floured surface, roll the dough to a ¼-inch thickness.

Put the broth back on the heat and bring to a rolling boil. Cut the rolled-out dough into 2- to 3-inch squares and drop them into the boiling broth. Stir occasionally to keep the dough from sticking together as it boils. After all the dough has been dropped in the pot, turn the heat down to low, and simmer the "pop-eye," lid *on*, for about 20 minutes. When it becomes irresistibly creamy and thickens up, it is ready for the feast!

Serves 6.

What love is to the heart, appetite is to the stomach.
The stomach is the conductor that leads and livens up the
great orchestra of our emotions.

—Gioacchino Rossini

Hit Me with Your Best Arrow

*B*efore the romantic movement in art, literature, and Hallmark cards turned him into an adorable, overfed, winged infant who flitted about indiscriminately wounding gods and humans with his potent arrows, Cupid (aka Eros, the Greek god of sexual love) was the unutterably sexy, strong, and handsome son of Aphrodite and Ares. So handsome was this god of love that his mother became disastrously jealous when one of his arrows struck the lovely mortal Psyche, rendering her instantly in love with him. His mother ordered him to make Psyche instead fall in love with the ugliest creature imaginable; upon glimpsing her, Cupid defiantly disobeyed.

Imagine a mother scorned. Aphrodite made Psyche her slave, imprisoned her, and subjected her to gross inhospitality. As the story goes, Psyche bribed someone in the goddess' court with two coins and two cakes (perhaps proving she was an independently wealthy, good cook) and by and by, overcame Aphrodite's wrath. Psyche eventually bore Cupid a daughter, and fittingly christened her Voluptas (Pleasure).

Somewhere in history, namely A.D. 269, the pagan celebration of this great lust story was transformed into the feast day of Saint Valentine, who was martyred by the Roman emperor, Claudius II on February 14. Today, the image of Cupid, the renegade archer with wings supercedes that of the saint.

When Cupid's quiver is emptied, the gold-tipped arrows inflame the victim with passion; those coated with lead create a frustrated, unrequited love deprived of all reason. With that in mind, let's envision what would happen if the arrows were dipped in chocolate: To borrow a phrase, "Without passion—and lovers' truffles—love cannot grow."

Lovers' Truffles

2 cups semisweet chocolate chips

½ cup whipping cream

2 teaspoons rum extract

½ cup powdered sugar

⅓ cup unsweetened cocoa

In a heavy saucepan on very low heat, melt chocolate chips with the whipping cream. Add rum extract and whisk until blended. Pour this sweet sludge into a pie pan and refrigerate for about an hour until the mixture is like soft fudge.

Sift the powdered sugar and cocoa together in a shallow bowl. Shape the fudge into balls using 1 tablespoon of chocolate mixture per ball. Roll the truffles in the cocoa and sugar mixture, and keep chilled until ready to serve. Nestle the truffles in a decorative candy box or display them on a crystal plate and present them to a paramour at a propitious time (after love making is always divine).

Makes approximately 2 dozen truffles.

Plant roses and lavender for good luck . . .
fall in love whenever you can.

—Alice Hoffman, *Practical Magic*

Need a Holiday?
Borrow One from a Good Pagan

You have to hand it to the early Christians for their improvisational conversion tactics when faced with a world of sun/earth/god/goddess-based, fertility-worshipping (and we all know what that entails—sex, sex, sex . . . oh, heavens!) heathens. Pagan vernal fertility festivals were celebrated in honor of Eastre or Eostra, the goddess of the dawn—the rebirth of the day. Do you see a connection here? Eastre—Easter? Appropriately, the annual Christian holiday commemorating the resurrection of Jesus Christ, thus the renewal of spirit, is always held on the first Sunday after the first full moon after the spring or vernal equinox.

As described in Scott Cunningham's *The Magic in Food,* to welcome the "breath of life" after a long, dark winter, rituals of food were performed to win the favor of the goddess Eastre. "Small, sweetened buns were baked and eaten to encourage the returning fertility of the earth. These ritual breads, created with carefully stored grain and honey, were marked with phallic symbols and visual representations of the sun's fertilizing influence upon the earth and humans . . . the phallic symbols, regarded with unnatural horror (by the Christians), were transformed into more 'seemly' crosses." We all know these breads are now eaten and given as gifts on Good Friday, the day of Christ's death.

The mystical qualities of the "hot phallic bun" have filtered into modern-day superstition. If eaten on Good Friday, it insures a year of good luck; sailors often keep one on board to prevent shipwrecks; it wards off evil and cures illness; it repels rats; and better yet, supposedly never goes moldy. I would imagine, if you put the time and focus into preparing the buns, marking them with whatever symbol you desire, your labors will be rewarded with gratitude and happiness, maybe even good sex.

Hot Cross Buns

5 teaspoons SAF-Instant yeast or 2 packages (7 grams) active dry yeast

1¼ cup lukewarm water

1 teaspoon plus ⅓ cup sugar

½ cup dried milk

½ cup melted butter or canola oil

1 teaspoon salt

1 teaspoon ground cinnamon

½ teaspoon ground cardamom

¾ teaspoon ground allspice

¼ teaspoon ground nutmeg

3 eggs, beaten

4½ to 5 cups unbleached white flour

1 cup golden raisins

½ cup currants or dried cherries, chopped and soaked in 3 table-spoons rum

1 egg whisked with 1 tablespoon water

Glaze of your choice

In a large mixing bowl, sprinkle 1 teaspoon of the sugar over ¼ cup of the lukewarm water. Let rest for a few minutes. Add additional all the yeast and remaining ⅓ cup sugar, the rest of the lukewarm water, dried milk, butter or oil, salt, spices, eggs, and half of the flour, stirring until a sticky dough begins to form. Add dried fruit and stir in remaining flour until dough is soft and warm but not sticky.

Turn out on a floured surface and knead. Replace the lightly-oiled dough in the bowl, cover with a damp cloth, and let rise in a warm spot until it just doubles in size (30 minutes or so, depending on the yeast; don't let dough overrise; see yeast information on page 35).

Grease a 10-by-15-inch jelly-roll pan. Punch dough down, remove from bowl, and allow to rest on the counter covered with inverted bowl for 10 minutes. Then, on a floured surface, knead again until dough is smooth. Divide dough into 20 to 24 portions and roll into balls. Place in pan and brush tops with egg whisked in 1 tablespoon water. With a sharp knife, slice a ⅛-inch-deep cross on top of each bun. Cover and let rise again until doubled in size (mark time for the future).

Preheat oven to 375°F. Bake for 20 to 25 minutes until golden brown. Prepare a glaze (see recipe for Butter Cream Frosting, page 103, and reduce by half). When buns are hot out of the oven, pour the glaze into the cross on the bun using the tip of a spoon. Serve warm.

Makes 20 to 24 pagan offerings to encourage a healthy dose of spring-fever frenzy or to ward off evil spirits lingering from the dark days of winter.

We can only receive what we're big enough to receive.
If we have small-sized hearts and souls we're going to get
puny angels, and if we can make our hearts bigger,
we're going to get bigger messengers.

—Matthew Fox

Some marriages are made in heaven—
but so are thunder and lightning.

—Anonymous

La Dolce Vita

*T*his cake cast a spell on me long ago. In my years of commercial baking, the Italian Cream Cake was the *only* cake I would ever agree to make for a wedding—it's my personal superstition. I truly believe that a bite of it brings good luck. If the bride wanted another flavor, I remained loyal to my idiosyncrasies and suggested she hire another baker. No one ever did. Rather, many a nervous bride gave an elated sigh when she entered the reception room and was greeted by this somewhat magical *torta*, while many a grateful—and of course lucky—groom took the cake in the face with a delighted grin.

This traditional Italian cake is served at sanctified celebrations of all types: birthdays, christenings, first communions, confirmations, and weddings. Because my recipe comes from Sardinia—the Island of Silence—my custom is to serve it garnished with Jordan almonds and fresh flowers and displayed upon the flat, handwoven, decorative raffia basket indigenous to that region of Italy.

When next you travel to Italy, whether physically or through astral projection, treat yourself to the enchantments of that seductive island and its people. If it is possible, try to bring home a few of these beautiful native baskets for your Italian Cream Cakes.

Italian Cream Cake

5 eggs, separated

1 cup butter, at room temperature

1⅓ cups sugar

1 teaspoon pure vanilla extract or rum

2 cups unbleached white flour

¾ teaspoon baking soda

½ teaspoon salt

¾ cup very finely ground almonds

1 cup plus 2 tablespoons buttermilk, at room temperature

Grease and flour a 10-inch springform pan or two 8-inch, round cake pans. Preheat oven to a notch between 325° and 350°F (set oven at 350°F if you live at 1 mile above sea level or higher).

Separate egg whites from yolks. Beat egg whites until peaks form; set aside.

In a large mixing bowl, beat butter, sugar, and vanilla together. Add 3 of the egg yolks (discard the other 2) and beat until smooth. Stir the flour, baking soda, and salt together in a separate bowl and fluff up a touch with a whisk (the goddess way of sifting). Then, alternately and slowly, add the flour mixture and buttermilk to the butter cream. Gently and attentively, blend in the ground almonds, and then, the egg whites.

Pour batter into prepared pan or pans and bake for 25 to 35 minutes or until a toothpick comes out clean. Cool completely before frosting with Butter-Cream Frosting (see page 103).

Serves 6 to 8.

A LA GODDESS

* Use your imagination when garnishing; I sometimes sprinkle angel flake coconut or sliced almonds over the frosted cake.

Come, let us dance, and make a feast of joy!

—Russian toast

A Vacation for a Cheesecake

*O*nce upon another lifetime, I ordered a slice of pumpkin cheesecake in a little restaurant on the outskirts of Burlington, Vermont. Suprisingly, I found myself fighting for the last forkfull of this spiced, intoxicating dessert with my friend Andrea's then-two-year-old daughter Erin (who is now a full-grown goddess).

Back in Colorado, baking away at Bonnie's on Aspen Mountain, I would actually find myself day-dreaming about that cheesecake. I wrote to the restaurant, addressing the baker, and shamelessly begged for the recipe. After a three-month silence, I received the recipe, handwritten on pink, lined paper. The baker, Julie, requested that I offer her accommodations when she visited Aspen in exchange for her recipe. My doors flew open! Though she never came to visit, and thus we never met, I have come to know her generosity of spirit every time I whip up this exceptional recipe.

I created my own tradition of serving this morsel of elementary magic every year on the fall equinox—a day for perfect balance of light and shadow, past and future, action and rest. When invited to a holiday gala, pumpkin cheesecake always headlines my contributions list. In the past, when I've sauntered into the party with some other offering, I've been met with the pouting faces of those who knew and hoped for this spicy treat.

Vermont Fall Equinox Pumpkin Cheesecake

Crust

2½ cups graham cracker crumb

¼ cup chopped nuts

2 tablespoons brown sugar

¾ teaspoon ground nutmeg

⅓ cup butter or margarine, melted

Filling

2¼ pounds cream cheese

1⅓ cups white sugar

2¼ cups brown sugar

2 tablespoons ground cinnamon

2½ teaspoons ground nutmeg

1½ teaspoons ground cloves

1 teaspoon ground ginger

6 eggs

⅔ cup evaporated whole milk or heavy cream

2¼ cups pumpkin purée, canned or cooked

2 tablespoons unbleached white flour

Topping

¾ cup chopped nuts of choice

1 teaspoon ground cinnamon

¾ cup brown sugar

3 tablespoons butter or margarine, chilled

Preheat oven to 350°F. Line the bottom of a 10-inch springform cheesecake pan with baking parchment paper. First make the crust by mixing all ingredients together, except the melted butter. Dribble the butter over the dry mixture, and, using a fork, mix together. Press the crust mixture into the prepared pan using the bottom of a glass or measuring cup. Bake the crust for 7 minutes and cool.

Reduce oven temperature to 300-315°F. Make the filling by whipping up the cream cheese until fluffy. Shake in sugars and spices and blend them into the cream cheese on low speed or by hand. Gently add the eggs, one at a time; add evaporated milk or cream and mix. Fold in the pumpkin and flour and blend well. Do not overmix. Pour the batter into the crust and bake for 70 to 80 minutes. (If there is extra batter, make a minicheesecake in a small loaf pan or muffin tin!)

While the filling is cooking, make the topping. With a fork, mix the nuts, cinnamon, and sugar together. Cut in the cold butter until crumbly. Keep chilled. (You will sprinkle this topping on the cheesecake after it has baked for 70 to 80 minutes; and then you will bake the cake 20 minutes more.) Taking care not to jiggle the cake, oh-so-gently sprinkle the topping over the cheesecake with as little interference as possible and gently shut the oven door. (Place a cookie sheet on the rack under the cake for this step to avoid a mess in the oven.) Bake for an additional 20 minutes.

(To check for doneness, touch the top with your finger and check "the jiggle effect." In the best cheesecakes, the less jiggle there is, the better. Trust your hunch. It should be done, but in case of doubt, leave the cake in for a few more minutes, and check again. Note the exact baking time for the next cheesecake. Baking times will differ depending on altitude, barometric pressure, and your oven.)

Remove from oven and let cool at room temperature for 24 hours before serving. Serve at room temperature or chilled.

Serves 10.

A la Goddess

* Leftovers (if there are any) should be refrigerated and will freeze well for up to a few weeks. Be prepared—this pumpkin cheesecake *will* put you in demand on holidays!

Why Make Such a Tzimmes
over Everything?

I playfully call the following recipe Drupe Stew, named after its secret ingredient, the plum, one of the hard-stoned, pulpy fruits of the almond family along with its cousins—apricots, peaches, and almonds. I've also heard it referred to as a "complicated Yiddish stew." C'mon, Tzimmes isn't so complicated—it's just an incredible wild combination of unlikely ingredients. I brew it up on Rosh Hashanah to celebrate yet another chance at a new year!

This recipe is from Mike Zwerdling, known to me simply as "Gail's dad," a popular pediatrician and obviously a kitchen demigod, as his stew proves. He notes, "The name is Tzimmes, which loosely translates to 'fun, excitement, brouhaha.'" Now, how could you *not* trust your child's doctor? Plan ahead—this stew is better reheated the next day.

Tzimmes

1½ pounds prunes, pitted

3 cups boiling water

2 tablespoons oil

3 pounds beef, cut into large cubes

2 onions, diced

1½ teaspoons salt

¼ teaspoon ground black pepper

3 sweet potatoes, peeled and quartered

4 carrots, peeled and sliced

½ cup honey

2 whole cloves or a pinch of ground cloves

½ teaspoon ground cinnamon

2 tablespoons fresh lemon juice

Wash the prunes, pour the boiling water over them, and soak for 30 minutes. Meanwhile, in a large heavy pot over medium-high heat, heat the oil and brown the beef and onions. Add the salt and pepper, reduce heat, and cook over low heat, covered, for 30 minutes.

Stir in the remaining ingredients, including the "prune water," and cook, covered, on low heat for an additional 1½ hours.

Serves enough fun and brouhaha for 6 people or more.

Dum vivimus vivamus

(Let us live while we live)

Cooking Up Candle Magic

Candles have been employed in almost every religious and spiritual tradition since fire was discovered. The flame symbolizes the energy of intention that is both released and attracted, and the light of the flame guides and illuminates these desires. The dripping wax represents the grounding power of the earth, while the dance of the flame resonates with the energy of manifestation. My home is rarely without the invocative glow of a candle.

Create an undisturbed space or altar—in the kitchen, bedroom, office—for purposeful candlework. Candles can be dressed with "holy water" or a favorite essential oil to enhance intent. They should always be properly grounded to insure safety in burning; candlesticks and votive glasses must be sturdy and secure. I usually set a seven-day votive (purchased from the Mexican food section of the supermarket) in a bowl of water, which serves both to ground the candle and create the Da, a powerfully creative and responsive energy dynamic invoked in West African magic. Always cleanse the candle holder—and its energy—in sea salt and water before burning a new candle in it; salt dispels miscued or troublesome energy.

Let me add one vital note: Be careful of what you ask for, because, if you have faith, you'll get it. Be wise.

Color	Attribute
Red	Love, passion, courage, vigor, invoking divine spirit
Orange	Concentration, healthy sexuality, emotional stability
Yellow	Attraction and creativity
Green	Abundance, wealth, health
Sky Blue	Intuition, peace
Indigo	Protection, clairvoyance, supernal vision
Purple	Power, divine power channelled from God/dess
White	Purification, clarity, blessing
Pink	Honor, friendship, gaiety
Silver	Serenity, moon meditation
Black	Release

A Soul, a Soul, for a Soul Cake

*T*rick or Treat? And *what are* you *going to be on Halloween?* It was on this night—All Hallow's Eve, the ancient Celtic fire festival of *Samhain* (pronounced "sow-ain")—that souls of the Underworld were said to return to visit or to seek retribution. Bonfires were lit to guide friendly spirits and keep sinister ones at bay.

Samhain was a ritual to secure a protected position between good and evil, the visible and the invisible, the sacred and the profane. So was the custom of "a-souling." Soul cakes—spicy shortbread biscuits or round spicy buns (the cake differed from village to village)—were baked on All Hallow's Eve and distributed to the hungry poor. They were also placed on the graves of the departed to offer nourishment to hungry souls. Children would seek these treats from house to house, singing,

> "A Soul, a soul, for a soul cake,
> Pray you good mistress, a soul cake."

Those crafty predecessors of our present-day trick-or-treaters would promise to offer prayers proportionate to each cake received. It was believed that through a sufficient quantity of prayer and food sacrifice, souls in limbo (a penitential wayside on the journey to heaven) would be freed from torment. This would, in turn, diminish the number of hauntings from lost souls wandering about when the sun came up on All Hallow's Day.

Has the balancing of these worlds—seen and unseen, light and shadowed—become insignificant in our technomodern times? Or has lore of spirit possession, divination, and the presence of intangible energies returned to reignite our imaginations? That is for each of us to say. Personally, I'm going to start mixing up my soul cakes right now, to get those hungry spirits pacified and sent on their haunting ways.

Halloween Soul Cakes

I cup butter, at room temperature

¾ cup sugar

I teaspoon grated lemon rind

½ teaspoon salt

½ teaspoon ground cardamom

½ teaspoon ground cinnamon

½ teaspoon ground ginger

½ teaspoon ground allspice

½ teaspoon ground nutmeg

I egg

2 tablespoons milk

3 cups unbleached white flour

½ teaspoon baking powder

Approximately 2 tablespoons apple juice

Sugar, currants, and slivered almonds for decorating

Cream the butter, sugar, lemon rind, salt, spices, egg, and milk together. Scrape the sides of the bowl and mix some more. Blend the baking powder into the flour and tap it into the creamed ingredients, stirring gently. Dribble in as much apple juice as necessary to form a workable, but not sticky, dough.

Preheat the oven to 350°F and line a cookie sheet with parchment. To form the soul cakes, either roll out the dough to ¼-inch thickness, cut impressions with a cookie cutter, and sprinkle sugar on top; or roll the dough into small balls and press to the same thickness with the buttered, sugar-coated bottom of a glass. Place the soul cakes on the cookie sheet, and press slivered almonds and currants onto the dough for decoration. Bake 7 to 10 minutes.

Makes approximately 2 dozen soul cakes.

෩෨

Hexenschaum (Witch's Foam)

This bewitching concoction is rumored to enhance powers of *thaumaturgy*—the ability to work miracles and magic—in the one who feasts upon it.

4 large apples

¼ cup water

2 tablespoons brown sugar

1 tablespoon white sugar

½ teaspoon cinnamon

Juice of 1 lemon

2 egg whites, stiffly beaten

½ cup cream, whipped

Ground nutmeg

Peel, core, and slice the apples. Stirring often, cook them over low heat in a covered, heavy-bottomed saucepan with water and sugars until the apples are tender. Stir in the cinnamon and lemon juice. Remove from heat and cool slightly. Purée gently in a blender or run the mixture through a sieve.

Fold the egg whites into the sieved apples and mix until thick and stiff. Serve *Hexenschaum* in a custard dish, topped with whipped cream and a dash of nutmeg.

Serves 4.

Any man who does not believe in miracles is not a realist.

—David Ben-Gurion

Fruit of the vine, Work of human hands,
May it become our spiritual drink.

—Blessing of the wine during Roman Catholic Mass

Cheer, Cheer for Fire Sign Wine

I learned to pray at a Notre Dame football game. You see, when I was a wide-eyed babe living in South Bend, Indiana, I adored tagging along with Dad to every "praise God for the tickets!" Notre Dame football game he attended. I was a privileged initiate basking in a wondrous secret society of tailgate parties, cheer chanting, and grownups acting like no other grownups I'd ever seen. I was in heaven . . . *Touchdown!* . . . Until the temperature dropped. The icy November winds that blow with a Michigan State vengeance off the shores of Lake Michigan will freeze your tears and tears there were. I cried and cried because I was so cold. So Dad would gather me in his big, toasty, parka-puffed arms, and cup my hands in his in prayer-finger form. We would pray for touchdowns and sing our cheer . . . and the tides would turn and our prayers would burn and I'd feel so warm and the ball was thrown . . . and touchdown! . . . at least we were warm. And Dad would pull out his little flask, raise it to the sky, and sip his holy wine.

It's been years since I sat on those old wooden bleacher seats, praying for sunshine and touchdowns. And when I close my eyes, I am in the safe embrace of my father's faithful tradition . . . the flask is now a thermos, and my fingers are now wise and warm, steadied by a hot mug of holiday *Glühwein*—glow wine—sparking the Irish-German fire in me with every sip. It's time for the game.

Fire Sign Wine

1 bottle (1.5 liter, 54 fluid ounces) full-bodied red wine (Burgundy or Beaujolais nouveau works nicely)

¾ cups sugar

3 cinnamon sticks, one partially grated

12 whole cloves and a pinch of ground cloves

½ teaspoon ground allspice

1 orange, juice and rind

1 lemon, juice and rind

1½ to 2 cups vodka (the stormier the weather, the more spirits are needed)

In a large, nonreactive saucepan, stir the wine, sugar, and spices together, grating part of one cinnamon stick over the mixture. Heat, covered, over very low heat while you cut the lemon and orange into 6 to 8 sections, squeeze the juice into the wine, and drop the segments of rind into the pot. Simmer for about 20 minutes or until wine is burning hot to the touch, but do not let it boil.

Add the vodka. When the potion is again almost too hot to taste-test, it is ready to drink. Serve in heat-tempered punch cups or glass mugs. I strongly urge that you take a seat before savoring this salubrious mulled tonic; it's healing effects will be felt with sizzling speed—especially when you leap up to cheer for the touchdown.

Warms up 4 to 6 adults.

Go, eat your food with gladness,
and drink your wine with a joyful heart.

—Ecclesiastes 9:7

A Grateful Goddess

For me at Thanksgiving, sweet potato pie is my personal favorite. Even the phrase *sweet-potato-pie* just lullabies from the lips in a sweet serenade. Like its first cousin, pumpkin pie (I have twenty-four different recipes for the "best-ever" pumpkin pie and am still dabbling with them to construct the u-l-t-i-m-a-t-e version—if you have it , send it in!), sweet earth-apple pie is a soulful requisite as the Thanksgiving—and Kwanza—dessert staple. This spicy, bourbon-spiked rendition of sweet potato pie is quite close to perfect.

Spiked Sweet Potato Pie

1 unbaked 9-inch pie shell (see page 104 for recipe)

3 sweet potatoes

½ cup white sugar

½ cup brown sugar

2 tablespoons butter, melted

⅔ cup evaporated milk

3 eggs

1½ teaspoons ground cinnamon

1 teaspoon ground nutmeg

½ teaspoon ground ginger

½ teaspoon ground cloves

¼ cup bourbon whiskey, or
   1 tablespoon pure vanilla extract

Bake the sweet potatoes at 350°F for one hour until very tender, then peel and mash them well. Prepare an unbaked pie shell, cover, and refrigerate.

Preheat oven to 400°F. In a large bowl, mix sweet potatoes and remaining ingredients together in the order listed until smooth and creamy. Pour this rich mixture into the unbaked pie shell. Place the pie in a 400°F oven and *immediately turn the temperature down to 350°F*. Bake for 45 to 55 minutes or until the center of the pie is set.

Serves 8.

I sometimes think the act of bringing food
is one of the basic roots of all relationships.

—The Dalai Lama

Give, and it shall be given to you.

—Luke 6:38

Kitchen Goddess Gift Giving

For whatever reason, the midwinter holidays inspire a generosity of spirit that fortunately becomes contagious, urging us all to share and give. As if a beguiling spell is poured over our hearts, we move about our days with genuine kindness, balmy contentment, and a serene openness to the needs and longings of others.

Why do we feel this transformative goodwill during the holidays? I like to think that we truly become caught in a transcendent enchantment: The collective energy of ancient, deeply spirited traditions has found its way into the present to give us a type of cosmic wake-up call. As the Yule song reminds us, "Hark! . . ." One of the first symptoms of the season is a growing itch to give gifts.

Giving gifts of food—food prepared with your touch, your thoughts, your spirit—carries a splendor of its own. Pies, cakes, cookies—with these gifts in hand, the giver easily traverses the shortest distance between the heart and the palate of the recipient. Creating lively, crunchy, nutty finger foods as gifts is fun, simple, and *appreciated*.

I have discovered that the mere mention of the word nut has a way of evoking uncanny passion in a person—pro or con, never neutral. Therefore, I recommend the following: First, try to ascertain the peculiarities of taste or allergy of an individual before you surprise him or her with nuts. Are almonds preferred over pecans? Pistachios over almonds? Talking nuts is a great topic of playful conversation, anyway. Second, be prepared: Make copies of these recipes to give with the gift, because I guarantee someone will ask you for them.

Sweet Celebrations of the Season

Owing its roots to ancient and universal custom, Thanksgiving, as we know it, was instated by our forefathers and mothers, the Pilgrims, in 1621, during their first successful harvest. Thanks to the local natives, a bountiful harvest was reaped and food was plentiful.

Annual harvest celebrations have fortified the human soul and psyche through antiquity. The Greeks honored the grain-giver, Demeter; Ceres, the Roman goddess of corn, received alms and prayers from the forerunners of the Italians. The mid-November Roman Feast of Jupiter honored the god of the heavens, his wife, and favored daughter with expensive, rich dishes and desserts—all tokens of prosperity. The eight-day Feast of the Tabernacles was the Hebrew way of thanking the powers that be for the super-abundance of harvest and prosperity.

Symbolically, the dishes that are set before us on the Thanksgiving table are themselves sacrifices. Though sincerely grateful for Grandma's slow-roasted, cornbread-stuffed, butter-basted turkey with all the trimmings, we may have a low-grade case of temporary amnesia when it comes to being actively aware of the origins of the feast. Without a working partnership between humankind and the goddesses of grain, nature, and the perpetual cycles of life, we'd miss our "just desserts."

Holiday Spiced Nuts

2 cups water

8 cups sugar

2 tablespoons salt

¼ cup plus 4 teaspoons
ground cinnamon

4 teaspoons ground nutmeg

4 teaspoons ground cloves

4 pounds shelled nuts (almonds
and pecans are my favorites)

In a very large, heavy saucepan, cook water, sugar, salt, and spices over medium heat until the mixture reaches the soft-ball stage (235–240°F; after being dropped in cold water, the syrup can be shaped into a ball, but flattens when removed from water). Remove from heat and stir in the nuts, using long, slow, sweeping motions, until all are completely covered.

Cover a surface with waxed paper, dump the nuts onto the paper, and separate the clumps by pulling them apart. Let these wildly spicy nuts cool before dividing them among decorative gift jars or serving bowls.

Makes approximately 10 cups.

Pistachio Brittle

I cup water

I cup brown sugar

I cup white sugar

I cup corn syrup

I teaspoon salt (omit if nuts
are salted)

2 cups raw or roasted pistachios,
shelled

I teaspoon pure vanilla extract

2 tablespoons butter

¼ teaspoon baking soda

Prepare a well-buttered surface or a baking pan lined with parchment paper (thus you will avoid saucepans full of frustration). In a large, heavy saucepan bring the water to a boil. Reduce heat and stir in the sugars. Then stir in the corn syrup, and cook to hard-ball stage (250°F).

Add salt if necessary. Stir occasionally. If you're using raw pistachios, add them now, before cooking the brittle to the hard-crack stage (295–310°F). If you are using roasted pistachios, add them later. Remove the saucepan from heat and gently stir in vanilla, butter, and baking soda, and, if they are roasted, add the pistachios last.

Immediately but slowly, pour the concoction onto the well-buttered surface or parchment-lined pan. With a buttered wooden spoon or spatula, spread the brittle out over the surface. Pick up the brittle (grease your hands or wear cotton gloves), turn the entire slab over, and pull very gently in alternating directions—lengthwise, then widthwise—until it is transparent. When completely cooled, crack into bite-sized pieces and store in a lined, airtight tin.

Makes about 1½ pounds of knock-out brittle.

A la Goddess

* I often break the brittle up into miniature pieces and use it in cookie dough. By creatively employing the Margie's Ultimate Chocolate Chip Classics recipe (page 56), a playful kitchen goddess can contrive a wonderful pistachio toffee cookie! Instead of the chocolate chips, add 2 cups of brittle to the recipe. Also, try to use fresh, farm-harvested nuts when possible.

I bring you good news of great joy . . .

—Luke 2:10

A Christmas Story

To borrow and adapt a phrase from my brother, "The world is divided into two types of people—those who have made a Christmas stollen, and those who have not." Authentically named *Dresdner Christstollen*, or "Baby Jesus' swaddling clothes," this traditional German coffeecake brightens our table every Christmas. Its creation, however, insists on a focused baking prowess as no other recipe does.

My brother and I regressed to the sibling rivalry of six-year-olds when making this labor of love one particular holiday. Mike insisted on making his version of the stollen, which meant lacing it with marzipan; I saw that as much too bothersome. The defining moment came when we tried to find this ground-almond delicacy on a Christmas Eve in Maquoketa, Iowa. Mary, Joseph, and the Baby Jesus himself would have had an easier time finding an inn in Bethlehem than they would have had finding marzipan in Maquoketa!

Thus, my favored marzipan-free, braided version of *Christstollen* graced the blessed breakfast table. Nonetheless, we agree wholeheartedly on the splendor of the rest of the recipe.

Brother Mike's Sunrise Stollen

2 cups milk

5 teaspoons SAF-Instant dried baker's
yeast or 2 packages active dry yeast

¼ cup lukewarm water

½ cup sugar

½ cup butter or margarine,
at room temperature

3 eggs

1 teaspoon salt

1 teaspoon ground cardamom

¾ teaspoon ground cinnamon

8 to 8½ cups unbleached flour

1 cup currants or golden raisins,
soaked in ¼ cup rum

1 cup sliced almonds

½ cup candied citron

½ cup chopped dried apricots or
dried cherries

Marzipan (optional)

The Glaze

2 cups powdered sugar

3 tablespoons milk or 1 tablespoon
orange juice plus 2 tablespoons milk

Scald the milk and set it aside to cool. Sprinkle yeast over the warm water and set the mixture aside. In a large bread bowl, combine the cooled milk with sugar and butter or margarine, and mix well. Separate 1 egg (reserving the white for the glaze). Add the yolk and remaining 2 whole eggs, salt, cardamom, cinnamon, and 4 cups of the flour. Stir gently, add dissolved yeast mixture, and stir in currants or raisins, almonds, citron, apricots or cherries, and the remaining flour to texture. When you're feeling the "burn" from stirring (about 5 minutes), turn the dough onto a lightly floured surface and knead a few times. Let it rest, covered, in a warm, greased bowl until it doubles in size (SAF-Instant yeast takes about 35 minutes; approximately half the time of regular yeast; see ordering information on page 35).

After the dough has risen, punch it down, and knead it lightly again. If your tradition is to prepare the stollen on Christmas Eve and bake it early Christmas morning, place the dough back in the bowl, cover it, and refrigerate overnight for up to 12 hours. If you choose to omit the refrigeration step, proceed directly to the kneading, shaping, and second rising.

Divide the dough into 3 portions for a braided loaf or 2 portions for an oblong, marzipan-filled loaf, and knead until the pieces are shiny and elastic. To make a braid, roll and squeeze the dough into 18-inch long ropes and braid them together, tucking the ends under. For 18-inch-long oblong loaves, press the dough flat, line the center with marzipan, and fold the dough around the filling. Place on a parchment-lined or greased baking pan, the loaf seam-side down, cover with a warm, damp towel, and let rise until the stollen has swelled nicely and looks ready to bake.

Preheat oven to 350°F. Brush stollen with beaten egg white and bake for 30 to 40 minutes, until golden and hollow-sounding when tapped. Serve stollen warm, either heavily dusted with powdered sugar or drenched in plenty of glaze. (Mix powdered sugar with milk (or milk and juice) to form glaze.)

Serves 12.

A great and wondrous vision appeared . . .
a woman clothed with the sun, and the moon under her feet,
and upon her head a crown of twelve stars.

—Revelation 12:1

"Here's to Those Who Love Us Well . . ."

I never—not once—in my life saw my Grandma Beiser cook. The only fare I ever saw in her refrigerator was "hops and barley sandwiches"— beer. Yet my most vivid recollection is seeing her, relaxing at her retro 1960s formica-topped, chrome dinette kitchen table (a touch scarred from forgotten burning cigarettes), her luminous blue eyes sparkling mischievously, accompanied by an admirer or two—an uncle, an aunt, a gentleman friend, a cousin, a person from church, a nun or a priest, the cleaning lady—drinking a beer. Grandma Beiser ruled her world from her kitchen with laughter and outpourings of her philosophies, her scepter a Hamm's, a Schlitz, or a Pabst Blue Ribbon.

Describing her as "outspoken" would be a diluted understatement in reference to Margaret Penning Beiser. She possessed that dangerously delightful quality of speaking her mind with a knife's-edge honesty, either leaving you quaking or smiling in the aftermath of her diatribes. In response to the ever-present dust enshrouding her cabinets, Grandma would proclaim, "If my friends are coming to see my housekeeping instead of me, they may just as well stay home." Her best kitchen advice, "If guests are coming and the dishes are dirty, put them in the oven."

Uncle Dave, Grandma's eldest, says Grandpa did most of the cooking. Mom remembers, as a young bride married to the middle child, my father, that it was Grandpa, not Grandma, who taught her how to grocery shop. Uncle Penny, the baby in the family, claims he was raised on cocoa and toast with real butter. Aunt Sue says Grandma's slow-cooked turkeys were legendary; that Grandma would get up in the middle of the night and baste that bird for hours and hours and hours. My brother Michael, her by-far-the-favorite grandson, tells of the times she cooked him bacon and eggs. I recall her fabulous ham on Thanksgiving and at Christmas, the two days they say she cooked.

She was graceful and complicated, frisky and demanding, wise and irreverent. Her brilliant wit and resilient humor transcended all the monkey wrenches fate tossed her way. The beautiful irony is that she was Queen of the Kitchen without ever having to raise a mixing spoon. But a glass she would raise—and often—and those of us who were lucky enough to share her world would see her smiling, azure eyes shine and hear her toast,

Here's to those who love us well,
And all the rest can go to hell.

I raise my fullest cup to Grandma Beiser—the most extraordinary kitchen goddess of all!

Grandma Beiser's Holiday Ham

1 ham (2 to 3 pounds), fully cooked and cured

1 can (20 ounces) pineapple rings; reserve liquid

1 can or bottle of beer

½ cup undiluted orange juice concentrate

1 cup brown sugar

1 teaspoon dry mustard

1 teaspoon ground cloves

1 teaspoon ground cinnamon

½ teaspoon ground nutmeg

Coarse cracked pepper

Preheat oven to 350°F. Place the ham in a large, greased baking pan and stab it about 10 times with a fork. Mix reserved pineapple juice and orange juice concentrate with the beer and pour about three-fourths of this "secret blend" marinade over the ham. Combine the brown sugar and the spices and sprinkle them over the ham. Slap the pineapple rings on top of everything. Lightly drizzle the rest of the "secret blend" over the ham, taking care not to wash everything away. Put it in the oven and cook, uncovered, for 45 minutes to an hour (about 20 minutes per pound) or until a meat thermometer registers 140°F. Baste several times if you remember. If the ham is browning too much, drape a piece of tin foil over it.

When it's done, turn the oven off and let the ham rest in the oven until you are ready to serve it. If for any reason guests don't get around to eating it, slice and serve in sandwiches for the next few days.

Serves 6 to 8.

One More Reason to Celebrate

Just when you're doing the dishes after the Thanksgiving feast, taking down the Christmas tree, or beginning to feel the postpartum blues of the big birthday party, remember, *somewhere* on earth someone is celebrating *something*. And for each feast, celebration, or holiday, there are customs to honor, traditions to keep, and offertory plates and glasses to fill. Here are some of my favorites.

6 January	Epiphany
13 January	Celtic Brew-Fest
22 January	Feast of the Kitchen God (Chinese)
24 January	Blessing of the Happy Woman's Candle (Hungarian)
1 February	Feast Day of Goddess-Saint Bridgid (Irish/Celtic/Catholic)

9 February	Feast of Apollo
4 March	Feast of Rhiannon (Welsh)
20–21 March	Spring Equinox
25 March	Lady Day; Return of the Goddess
1 May	May Day; Beltane Fire Fertility Festival
21 June	Summer Solstice
10 July	Lady Godiva Day (English)
19 July	Wedding of Adonis and Aphrodite (Greek)
22 July	Feast Day of Saint Mary Magdelene
1 August	Lammas, the First Harvest
15 September	Birthday of the Moon (Chinese)
22–23 September	Autumn Equinox
29 September	Michaelmas, Feast of Saint Michael the Archangel
2 October	Feast of the Guardian Angels and Spirits (Catholic/Druidic)
4 October	Feast of Saint Francis of Assisi; World Day for Animals
31 October	Samhain Eve; Halloween
6 December	Saint Nicholas Day
20 December	Mother Night
21 December	Yule; Winter Solstice

So feel free to celebrate!

CHAPTER 8

The Golden Apple Invitational

Dost thou think, because thou art virtuous,
there shall be no more cakes and ale?

—Shakespeare, *Twelfth Night*, II, 3

Good Goddess, Let's Play!

Gather three of the great Greek goddesses—Hera, Athena, and Aphrodite—at the same party, get the energy stirring among them, and arrange a beauty contest that calls for the fairest to emerge triumphant and glorified. The Judgment of Paris involved such a contest—a soap opera vanity fest— that resulted in war and the division of heaven. All over an apple . . . not just any apple, of course, but a *golden* apple. A golden apple inscribed "For the fairest." At the height of jubilation during the wedding feast of the King of Thessaly and his sea nymph, a slighted minor goddess who was not invited, Eris, the goddess of discord and strife, took revenge. She tossed the fabled fruit into the midst of these three goddesses, and each immediately claimed that the prize was definitely and deservedly hers. A turbulent three-sided tug-of-war ensued. Zeus was called to preside over the decision of who would win the apple.

Of course, Zeus took one look at his wife, his daughter, and his occasional lover and retreated. The ladies were then led by Hermes to the strikingly handsome shepherd Paris, who was enlisted to judge the beauty pageant. The three goddesses hit him with their best bribes: Hera offered him power over all the kingdoms of Asia; Athena promised him victory in all his endeavors and battles; the frisky, cunning Aphrodite merely told him she would make any woman he wanted fall in love with him. If you were a man, who would you pick?

A man he was, and so the goddess of love danced away with the golden apple. The passion-infused Paris—though he was supposedly contentedly married—then chose another man's wife, Helen of Troy, the most beautiful mortal in Greece. His judgment thus incited the Trojan war and Mount Olympus was rocked to its soul. Three powerful deities—Apollo, Ares, and Artemis—sided with Aphrodite and the Trojans; the "Hera-and-Athena's Aphrodite Hate Club" enrolled Hermes, Poseidon, and Hephaestus (her cuckolded ex-husband). Nevertheless, the golden goddess Aphrodite had her coveted recognition . . . and her apple, which forevermore would become that great symbol of dangerous, delicious, undaunted passion.

And what did this fair goddess do with her apple? Share it with Eve? Snow White? Her teacher? I say she whipped up an incomparably scrumptious dish and entered her recipe into the The Golden Apple Invitational, a virtual playground of spirited cooking. Inspired by Aphrodite's delicious wit and saucy spirit, I share the following recipe.

Golden Apple Dumplings

Dough

2 cups unbleached white flour

1¼ teaspoons salt

¼ teaspoon baking powder

½ cup *cold* Crisco shortening

⅓ cup *cold* margarine or butter

⅓ cup *ice* water

Apple Bath

8 cups water

1½ cups white sugar

1½ cups brown sugar

¼ cup butter

1 tablespoon ground cinnamon

2 teaspoons ground nutmeg

Apple Filling

½ cup golden raisins

1 tablespoon rum

1 cup raw sugar

1 tablespoon ground cinnamon

1 teaspoon ground nutmeg

6 Golden Delicious apples, cored and peeled

2 tablespoons butter, cold and cut into cubes

Make the dough first. Blend dry ingredients together. Cut in the shortening and margarine or butter with a fork or pastry cutter until you achieve a fine, crumbly texture. Dribble the ice water over the mixture and mix together with a fork or by quickly and lightly tossing with your hands. Without touching the dough too much (the warmth of your hands will make it tough when baked), form an oblong piece of dough. Wrap with plastic and refrigerate until you are ready to use it.

In a large, heavy saucepan, bring all the ingredients of the Apple Bath to a rolling boil, stirring it often. After the elixir has boiled for a few minutes, turn the heat down and simmer for about 15 to 20 minutes. When the Apple Bath begins to thicken, taking on the consistency of maple syrup, turn the heat off but leave the saucepan on the stove while preparing the filling and the golden dumpling orbs.

To prepare the filling, soak the raisins in rum. In a separate bowl, mix the sugar and spices together.

Preheat the oven to 400°F. To create the dumplings, roll the dough into a ⅛-inch-thick rectangle on a well-floured surface. Without measuring too meticulously, cut dough into 6 approximately 5-by-5-inch squares. Place a cored and peeled apple in the center of each square. Fill each apple with 1 tablespoon of the sugar and spice mixture followed by a spoonful of drunk raisins, followed again by a spoonful of sugar and spice mixture, and topped with a teaspoon of butter. As if wrapping a package, bring the four points of the dough together atop the apple and glue them shut with cold water.

Place the orbs an inch apart in an ungreased 13-by-9-by-2-inch or larger baking dish, and pour the Apple Bath around—not on—the dumplings until the bottom halves of the dumplings are relaxing in approximately 1½ inches of liquid.

Bake at 400°F in the lower half of your oven for 15 minutes. Reduce the heat to 350°F and cook for another 35 to 45 minutes, until the orbs are golden brown. Pierce with a fork to check doneness. (Drape tinfoil over the tops of the dumplings if they begin to darken too intensely.)

Serve the warm dumplings in beautiful—crystal, if possible—individual dishes, topped with a luxurious portion of the bath, and graced with a scoop of premium vanilla ice cream.

Makes 6 dumplings. To the fairest!

**Be silent no more,
Enchantress wake again!**

—Sir Walter Scott

*It's a funny thing about life; if you
refuse to accept anything but the best,
you very often get it.*

—W. Somerset Maugham

Who Has the Fairest Recipe of Them All?

The Golden Apple Invitational serves up an opportunity for you to share *your* heavenly recipes, spirited stories, and saucy secrets. What are *your* favorite concoctions? Do you have a delicious secret or a spirited story that adds spice to your recipe? What does being a goddess in the kitchen mean to you? Who is or are the goddess or goddesses that you hold close to your heart and how is this source of inspiration manifested in your life? I welcome every letter, thought, recipe, story, desire, spell, and secret. Let's tell our tales, open our souls, and share our ingredients of life!

The Golden Apple Invitational invites recipes of any kind—for beverages, appetizers, soups, salads, entrées, desserts, even recipes for dog biscuits if you have a great one! In honor of the wise and worldly goddess Athena, I'd be particularly interested in ethnic and international fare. Of course, any creation that is unique, original, or unabashedly delicious is most welcome.

My own Golden Apple wish list includes elusive recipes that I have, for whatever reason, whimsically coveted throughout the years. Perhaps you have the recipe or can persuade the person who does know it to share it!

These creations include:

* The taffy apple pie from the Gold Rush Restaurant in Bloomington, Indiana

* Peggy Tavener's (aka Lady Margaret) cheesecake with lemon curd topping

* A splendid chocolate chip pound cake with maple glaze

* The jicama sweet potato pancakes from a Vermont inn that members of the Grateful Dead so enjoyed

* The crème brûlée from La Ferme Restaurant in Genoa, Nevada

* Princess Diana's favorite ginger-rhubarb muffins from the Harbour Club in London

* Juanita's Springerle

* The recipe for caldereta de langosta—a seafood lobster stew—from Es Pla restaurant on the island of Minorca

* Faith's tiramisu

* A savory, traditional booyaw, purpoo mulligatawny, or hotchpotchsoppa

* Any recipe that is a personal, if-I-were-on-a-deserted-island-and-could-only-taste-one-thing favorite

So, my friends, come to the goddess party and feast on the fun! I would love to hear from you. Simply send your heavenly recipe—highlighted by a spirited *Romancing the Stove* story—to:

THE GOLDEN APPLE INVITATIONAL

c/o Margie Lapanja

P. O. Box 5515

Incline Village, NV 89450

www.ekstaza.com

www.foodthatrocks.com

May the call of the goddess keep your minds
emblazoned with light and grace,
and may you continue to stir up delicious fun
in the kitchen and in life.
Stay in touch!

Acknowledgments

I am forever grateful to Claudia Schaab, for her original vision, enthusiasm, and easy laughter, and of course for picking my proposal out of the slush pile;

To everyone at Red Wheel/Weiser and Conari Press for their waterfall of faith and support in this endeavor;

To Leslie Berriman, my goddess-editor, and Brenda Knight for holding the light;

To Mary Jane Ryan for giving the best advice this writer could ever hear, "Go wild; go fun!";

To all my goddess friends, Shivani, Ambrosia, Cindy, Cathy, Shannon, Paula Wilson, Donna O., Linda, Chyrise, Kelly, Cassidy, Maria Girsch, Kitty, Nena Marina Girsch, Susan S., Grace, Kathryn G., Kimmy T., Peggy Tavener, Liz, Kim K-T., and Christa, thank you for playing with me; to Dragica Lapanja, Patty Eikam, and Patrice Patterson Parsons for support and energy;

To Colleen O'Brien, the Scorpio writer with an editor's pen;

To each one of you who shared your recipes, secrets, lives, stories, and your light, you are definitely on the list in my heart;

To Bonnie Brucker Rayburn, who taught me to bake, and Liz Riseden, who taught me to write;

To my favorite demigods,
Wayne Pate, Chuck Chejfec, Peter Quah, Terry Little, and Brewmaster Fred;

To Joe Beiser, my dad, for coming to me between the lines and
in dreams and during my hikes, always to inspire and encourage,
"Listening to you, I get the music . . .";

To my adoring twin brother and miracle man, Michael Joseph,
who was always quick and generous with those three little words,
and to "Sistar" Kate, for her letters, for listening,
and for her translations of the human heart and soul;

To Vojko Lapanja, *prijatelj-ljubimec-soprog-polbog*,
Slovenian ski champ, and dashing dad extraordinaire, who dauntlessly accepted
the role of Lila's food and entertainment committee so I could accomplish
whatever goddessing needed to be done; I cherish *you*;

To Lila Grace, blossoming goddess, wild woman, and muse;

To Denyse Hafner Hughes, my mom.

Index

About the Author

Margie Lapanja, author of *The Goddess' Guide to Love* and *Food Men Love*, is a food enthusiast and "aphrodisiac expert" who holds a degree in behavioral sciences and humanities. A former magazine food editor, restaurant critic, and professional baker, she has appeared on national television and radio programs demonstrating trade secrets and discussing favorite topics of FOOD and LOVE by exploring the positive and revitalizing effects of food on the mind, body, and spirit. She enjoys life at Lake Tahoe in Nevada with her husband and their daughter.

To Our Readers

onari Press publishes books on topics ranging from spirituality, personal growth, and relationships to women's issues, parenting, and social issues. Our mission is to publish quality books that will make a difference in people's lives—how we feel about ourselves and how we relate to one another. We value integrity, compassion, and receptivity, both in the books we publish and in the way we do business.

As a member of the community, we donate our damaged books to nonprofit organizations, dedicate a portion of our proceeds from certain books to charitable causes, and continually look for new ways to use natural resources as wisely as possible.

Our readers are our most important resource, and we value your input, suggestions, and ideas about what you would like to see published. Please feel free to contact us, to request our latest book catalog, or to be added to our mailing list.

CONARI PRESS

An imprint of Red Wheel/Weiser, LLC

P.O. Box 612

York Beach, ME 03910-0612

800-423-7087

www.conari.com